The Real Taste of Latin America
A CULINARY TOUR

Text by Gonzalo Monterroso

Recipes by Diana Boudourian

Warwick Publishing

The Real Taste of Latin America
(Cocina Latinoamericana)
©2004 Bifronte S.R.L.

We acknowledge the financial support of the Government of Canada through the Book Publishing Industry Development Program for our publishing activities.

ISBN: 1-894622-35-9

Warwick Publishing Inc.
161 Frederick Street, Toronto, Ontario M5A 4P3 Canada
www.warwickgp.com

Distributed by
CDS
193 Edwards Drive
Jackson TN 38301 USA
www.cdsbooks.com

Printed and bound in Canada

General Editor
Sonia Passio

Geographic Photography
Agencia Comesaña

Guest Photographers
Carlos Mordo
Ron Lovelace
Florencia Podestá
Marcela Navone
Rafael Ruiz
Focus

Food Photography
Jorge Luis Campos

Backgrounds of the dishes
Martín Gómez Álzaga

Cover Photograph
Martín Gómez Álzaga

Text
Gonzalo Monterroso

Recipes
Diana Boudourian

Design
Sonia Passio

Mac Operator
Duilio Molina

Assistant Publisher
Rosa Achugar

Recipe Proofreading
Gabriela Fernández

Proofreading
M.B.L.L.

Back Cover
Enrique Limbrunner

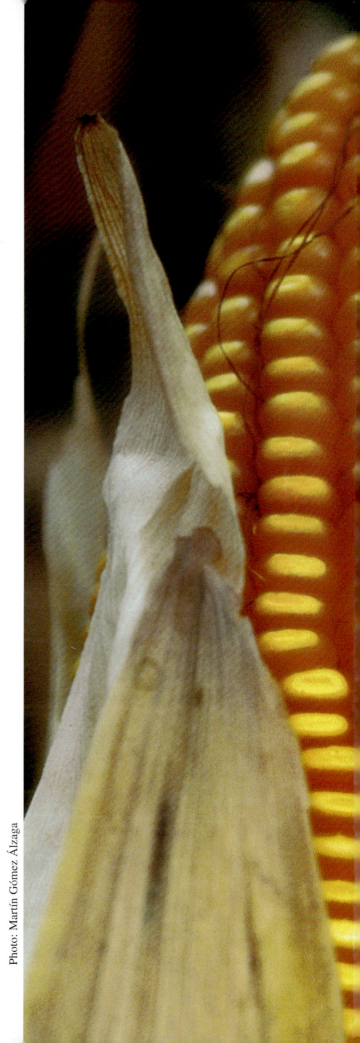

Photo: Martín Gómez Álzaga

Contents

MEXICO

The Castle, Chichen Itza, Yucatan, Mexico Photo: Panoramic Images

From the moment we entered the homes we found so many roosters and hens, cooked in the way the Indians eat them, with their peppers and cornbread, which they call tamales, that on the one hand we wondered at such a novelty and on the other we rejoiced at the large amount of food.

—Bernal Díaz del Castillo, chronicler of the conquest of Mexico

*I*f you look at the map of Mexico with a bit of imagination, you will see that it is shaped like a cornucopia, a horn of plenty, a decoration always depicted as overflowing with produce. Historically influenced by two oceans, Mexico comprises the same mix of warm, temperate, and cold lands as found in the Andean countries. The two Mexican mountain ranges embrace the highlands where the Aztecs ruled of old; the Spaniards preferred their cuisine to that of any other nation in the Americas.

The Aztecs ate tortillas, tamales, and meats prepared with sauces; they drank cocoa, *atoles*, and *pulque*. At the markets there was an abundance of corn, beans, and peppers of different varieties and colors, red tomatoes (*jitomate*, from *xictomatl*: navel tomato) and green tomatoes (*miltomate*), squash flowers and seeds (still eaten in stews, tacos, and soups), all kinds of fruits and sweets, fermented maguey (agave) juice, and pipes for smoking (*cañas de humo*).

At first the Europeans were given a friendly welcome. They were entertained with official banquets at which, according to the chroniclers, an army of cooks served Emperor Montezuma over thirty native stews warmed on braziers. The Spaniards learned to drink foamy chocolate from calabash cups and to smoke tobacco after their meals.

But when the Aztecs realized that Hernán Cortés intended to take possession of their land, the banquets came to an end, and Cortés's men were reduced to pilfering rations of corn, beans, and squash, never missing at the people's table. This sacred nutritional trilogy remains fundamentally unchanged to this day. In fact, one of the intriguing aspects of Mexican cuisine is the extent to which the pre-Hispanic influence has endured. Many corn-based dishes follow the ancestral recipes, including the use of the *metate* or grinding stone, the Aztec version of a blender. Corn, the main American contribution to the world diet, was both a daily source of nutrition and a ritual food. Both the ears of corn (*elotes*, the base for soups and stews), and its delicious fungi (*huitlacoches*) were used. Corn flour was used to prepare *tortillas, tamales,* and the beneficial *atole,* a kind of soupy

Photo: Florencia Podestá

Palenke,
Mexico.

cornmeal mush — which, miraculously, nobody complains about. This type of porridge became a crossbreed when it was sweetened with *panela* (brown sugar) and flavored with cinnamon and served as a beverage.

Meat rations — stewed, roasted, or cooked in a hole in the ground — gave the diet some variety. Domestic animals (turkeys and small dogs) were fattened, and at the market there were poultry, fish, and even insects, fried or stewed, such as *chapulines* (crickets), *chinicuiles* (maguey worms), and *escamoles* (ant's eggs), considered the Mexican caviar. The taste for the meat of the iguana — which, according to chronicler Fernández de Oviedo "is much better to eat than to look at" — survives in the iguana fricassee from Guerrero and in the Campeche stew.

Tortillas are made with different types of corn and come in different sizes

Mole Poblano (Mexico) #1

INGREDIENTS
(Makes 4 servings)
4 chicken breasts
4 cups vegetable broth
½ onion, chopped
2 cloves garlic,
   crushed
salt and pepper

MOLE
1 *pasilla* chile
1 *poblano* chile
1 wide chile
1 mulatto chile
½ onion
2 cloves garlic
1 flour tortilla

1 cup almonds
⅓ cup seedless golden
   raisins
⅓ cup seedless black
   raisins
3 squares unsweetened
   chocolate
1 clove

1 tsp. ground
   coriander seeds
1 tsp. anise seeds
4 tsp. sesame seeds
½ tsp. cinnamon
1 slightly green
   banana
4 Tbsp. lard

PREPARATION

Cook the chicken breasts in the broth together with half an onion, chopped, and 2 cloves of garlic, crushed. Add salt and pepper and boil for 30 minutes over medium heat. Remove from heat and set aside, leaving everything in the broth.

MOLE

Follow one of the methods for "Preparing Chiles" below. Peel them, removing the seeds and inner membranes, and, using a food processor, chop them along with half an onion and the remaining 2 cloves of garlic. Set aside. Break the tortilla into four pieces, slice the banana and process both together with the peeled almonds, raisins, anise seeds, cinnamon, ground coriander, 2 tsp. sesame seeds and clove.

Fry this mixture in lard for 5 minutes over medium heat, adding the processed chiles and stirring constantly to prevent the mixture from sticking to the bottom of the pan. Add a cup of broth to make the sauce thinner.

Add the chocolate in small pieces and stir with a wooden spoon until it melts and the sauce thickens.

Add the breasts and cook over low heat for 10 minutes, adding broth if necessary.

Sprinkle the remaining sesame seeds over the chicken breasts and mole and serve.

Preparing Chiles (Hot Peppers)

There are several ways to peel the chiles; the traditional way is to expose them to the flame of the stovetop burner, turn them until the skin blisters and scorches slightly, and then place them in a plastic bag for 10–15 minutes. Then they are peeled carefully to avoid breakage.

They can also be microwaved at High, turning them over after 5 minutes.

The procedure for peeling them is the same in all cases, *placing them in a plastic bag first.*

To temper the flavor of the chiles, remove the seeds and inner membranes and then soak them in water and vinegar, changing the solution several times.

Remember that contact with the skin produces a burning sensation. Wear surgical gloves as you work; otherwise, you should wash your hands with water and baking soda immediately after handling the chiles.

Degree of Piquancy
(Hottest first)
Habanero
Tabasco
Chiltepín and *Piquín*
Manzano
De Arbol
Serrano
Jalapeño
Poblano
Pasilla

Flour Tortillas (Mexico) #2

INGREDIENTS

(Makes 6 tortillas)

2 cups all-purpose flour

½ tsp salt

½ tsp dry yeast

½ Tbsp lard

½–¾ cup water

PREPARATION

Mix the flour, salt, and dry yeast in a bowl. Add the lard and the water, both at room temperature, and knead until you get a homogeneous dough. Divide in 6 portions. To shape the tortillas, place each portion between two sheets of waxed paper or plastic wrap to prevent them from sticking and press them between the palms of your hands or with a rolling pin until you get thin discs about 6 inches in diameter. Heat a thick-bottomed pan, remove the wax paper or plastic wrap and cook each tortilla for a couple of minutes on each side over medium heat until the edges start curling up and look slightly golden.

TIPS
In order for the tortillas to be evenly cooked, the pan must be very hot. You can also use a plain pancake griddle.

Corn Tortillas (Mexico) #3

INGREDIENTS

(Makes 6 tortillas)

2 cups harina de

maíz (corn flour — *not* cornmeal)

½–¾ cup water

1 tsp salt

PREPARATION

Follow the procedure for flour tortillas. If the dough is sticky, add a little flour and continue working it. If, on the other hand, it is too dry, slowly add a little water to moisten it and continue working it until it becomes smooth and homogeneous.

NOTE
Flour or corn tortillas can be cut in quarters and fried (nachos); they are a delicious garnish for any dish. It is important not to overcook the tortillas or they will crack.

Quesadillas (Mexico) #4

INGREDIENTS
Flour Tortillas
Grated Oaxaca, mozzarella or Cheddar cheese

PREPARATION

Warm each tortilla in an ungreased pan for one minute over medium heat to soften it.

Fill the center of each tortilla with a mound of Oaxaca, mozzarella, or Cheddar cheese, fold it on itself and re-heat for one minute on each side over high heat until the cheese melts.

Alternate method of preparation: form a rectangle, fill it and fold the tortilla upwards on all sides, sealing the edges to keep the filling in; deep fry in oil or lard for 5 minutes over high heat.

---

and shapes. They are flattened with the palms of the hands and boiled or cooked by the fire; fried tortillas are clearly a Creole product, since the natives were not acquainted with fried foods. Tortillas were the first form of bread offered to Cortés to accompany meats stewed with *mole*. Centuries later, the tortilla continues to be an efficient tool to produce fast, filling snacks. There are plain tortillas (*chalupas, garnachas, panuchos, tostados,* and the ubiquitous *tacos*) or filled tortillas (*tlacoyos, quesadillas*); there is even a tortilla soup.

Tamales are, for many, the Mexican dish par excellence. These delicious pies, filled with stews and wrapped in corn or plantain leaves (depending on whether they are from the lowlands or the highlands) were votive and festive morsels in the times of Montezuma, when they were offered to the gods and to the poor alike.

According to Friar Bernardino de Sahagún, who lived in a Franciscan monastery in Tlatelolco during the second half of the 16th century,

Mancha Mantel *(Mexico) #5*

INGREDIENTS
(Makes 4 servings)
½ lb. pork sirloin
2 chicken breasts

2 cups vegetable broth
1 onion
2 tomatoes
2 wide chiles

1 green apple
1 plantain or slightly
    green banana
1 pear

2 peaches
1 Tbsp. sugar
lard as needed
salt and pepper

Boil the entire pork sirloin in vegetable broth for 20 minutes over medium heat; once the pork has taken on a light pink tint, add the chicken breasts, season with salt and pepper and continue cooking for another 10 minutes over medium heat.

Remove the meats, slice them and reserve the broth.

Remove the seeds and membranes from the chiles, and process them in a food processor together with the tomatoes and the onion. Fry the mixture in lard for 5 minutes at high and pour it into a saucepan.

Add the broth and the meat slices and boil for 10 to 15 minutes over medium heat.

Peel the apple, cube it and add it to the mixture. Continue cooking for 10 minutes.

Peel the banana, the pear and the peaches and cut them in small pieces; sprinkle them with sugar and add them to the mixture at the end of the cooking period.

Cook for another 5 minutes over medium heat and serve in individual bowls.

> TIP
> You may add flavor to the broth with coriander, oregano and mint leaves. The fruits should not be too ripe.

"the first thing that the host who was offering the feast or banquet did was make provisions for a great number of tamales to be made at his house, and determine what size they should be." This last detail is not trivial, since there are tamales that will fit in the palm of one hand, and others large enough to hold an entire suckling pig.

The regionalism of Mexican cuisine is evident in the vast geography of the tamale, which can withstand seemingly infinite variations in its fillings (meats, fish, vegetables, cheeses) and sauces (almost always ruled by hot peppers): there are peanut or hare tamales in Aguascalientes, squash or jerk beef tamales in Baja California, fish tamales in Campeche, vegetable tamales in Hidalgo, tomato and pine nut tamales in Chiapas, fish and mint tamales in Guerrero, catfish tamales in Morelos, shrimp tamales in Nayarit and Sinaloa, prickly pear and beef brain tamales in Zacatecas, cabbage tamales in Tabasco, anise tamales in Tlaxcala, stew tamales in Veracruz, ash tamales in Jalisco, black mole tamales in Oaxaca, *huasteco* tamales in Potosí, mourning tamales in Querétaro (made with black corn), cheese tamales (*corundas*) and corn tamales (*uchepos*) in Michoacán, and, last but not least, *chilpán,* the seven-chile tamales in Tamaulipas, and the variety of tamales from Yucatan.

Inseparable companions of tortillas are beans (refried, ground, stewed), whose empire has stood up to all conquests, having fed the inhabitants of America for the last five thousand years. Tomatoes and *chiles* (peppers) improved the flavors of indigenous cooking. Tortillas, tamales, and meats

Burritos (Mexico) #6

INGREDIENTS
(Makes 6 servings)
6 flour tortillas
1½ lb. beef

1½ cups vegetable broth
1 onion, chopped
2 cloves garlic, crushed
4 tomatoes, chopped
salt and pepper

GARNISH
2 red peppers, sliced and
fried in olive oil

PREPARATION

Prepare large flour tortillas, about 8 to 10 inches in diameter. Set aside.

Cook the beef in the vegetable broth, together with the chopped onion and crushed garlic, for 90 minutes over medium heat.

Add the chopped tomatoes and continue cooking for another 40 minutes over medium heat until the mixture thickens.

Break the beef up into very small pieces with two forks and season with salt and pepper. Mound a portion of the mixture in the center of each tortilla, folding each as a cone. Place the burritos on a serving dish and decorate with the red pepper slices, fried in olive oil.

> **NOTE**
> The filling may be prepared with chicken, fish, or pork to take advantage of any leftovers.

required mole (molli in the Náhuatl language), a pre-Hispanic purée that combines the best products of the native soil — chiles, beans, tomatoes — with contributions from lands beyond the sea (garlic, onions, and spices).

Just as the French claim to have a different type of cheese for each day of the year, the Mexicans can boast of preparing as many moles, as hot and dark as their chiles and chocolate will allow. The most famous is guacamole (avocado purée). The foreign guest would do well never to decline mole when offered, unless they want to cause an international incident!

As far as Mexicans are concerned, any dish is fine as long as it contains chiles, without which, according to Dominican missionary Bartolomé de las Casas, "Mexicans do not believe they are eating." There are about a dozen national varieties of chiles, besides the regional types. Oaxaca has at least six regional chiles. They are eaten fresh and dry or ground as a condiment. The chiles are used to prepare different foods and sauces that

Mexican Pork Sirloin *(Mexico) #7*

INGREDIENTS
(Makes 4 servings)
3 Tbsp. olive oil
1¼ lb. pork sirloin
1 onion, chopped
2 cloves garlic, crushed

MEXICAN SAUCE
2 *serrano* chiles
3 tomatoes
2 small avocados
1 lemon
1 onion, finely chopped
1 Tbsp. olive oil
1 Tbsp. grated cheese
salt and pepper

PREPARATION

Heat 3 Tbsp. of oil in a frying pan and brown the pork for 10 minutes — 5 on each side — over high heat, turning it to brown it evenly.

Add the chopped onion and crushed garlic. Cook on medium heat for 30 minutes, turning the meat every so often so that it cooks evenly.

Take the pork out of the pan, cut it in medium slices and cover with Mexican sauce.

MEXICAN SAUCE

Remove the seeds and the white membranes from the chiles, cut them in thin strips and soak them in hot water for an hour. Take them out of the water and set them aside.

Peel, seed, and cube the tomatoes and the avocados and place them in a bowl, sprinkling them with the juice of half a lemon. Add the onion, the chiles, the olive oil, and the grated cheese. Add salt and pepper and mix well.

Photo: Florencia Podestá

Church of Santo Domingo, Puebla, Mexico.

Photo: Carlos Mordo

Labna, Yucatan, Mexico.

the cookbooks classify according to their degree of piquancy. The most devilish are the chiles of the southeast (habanero chile, Tabasco chile).

The tomato is indigenous to Mexico and is celebrated daily in this country. When Leonardo da Vinci had only his humble cornmeal mush with cabbage to recommend, and long before it illuminated Mediterranean sauces, the tomato had already long enlivened the Aztec table.

Mexico City was built on the ruins of Tenochtitlán, the Aztec Venice that astonished Cortés in 1519. The canals of Xochimilco, a celebrated urban attraction, are part of that long gone imperial capital built on a lake. At Tlatelolco Square, where the last battle between the Aztecs and the Spaniards took place, there flourished a market (*tianquiz*) whose orderliness and profusion surprised the newcomers. According to

Bernal Díaz del Castillo, it was so large and well-attended "that it was impossible to see everything in two days."

In order to get an idea of what those Aztec markets looked like, visit the murals of Diego Rivera at the Palacio Nacional, which stands on the site of the ancient Palace of Montezuma where Cortés's retinue was greeted with cups of chocolate. The Catholic cathedral was erected upon the ruins of the temple of Quetzalcoátl.

The original tacos can be tasted at the Plaza de Armas, which they call Zócalo. For hundreds of miles you can find *carnitas, birrias, tingas* (stewed shredded beef), and regional broths like the *clemole* from Morelos and the *tlalpeño* from Michoacán, besides a battery of tamales, empanadas, tortillas, enchiladas, and *enfrijoladas*.

Many markets, like the one in Toluca, synthesize the whole gamut of national-al dishes, cooked before your eyes. The *antojitos* and fast foods are an ancient habit. Fray Bernardino de Sahagún got acquainted with them at the Tlatelolco market. If we are to believe the information recorded by Cortés — who confirmed his reputation for having a sweet tooth — the Aztecs already knew the concept of the restaurant ("There are houses where they give you food and drink for a price"). The Aztec menu consisted of cooked elotes (a Mexican ear of corn), poultry pies, empanadas, and fish stews. According to Father Sahagún, the food vendors "also sell barbecued meat, and meat roasted under the ground, that is, a kind of Mexican *curanto*."

If visitors like train travel, they should try getting to Mexico from Morelia (a showy provincial Baroque) or Veracruz, first and last Spanish redoubt in Aztec lands. There they cook the *olla veracruzana* — the regional stew — which confirms that the first heads of garlic, onions, and squash from Castile arrived at their destination. Before burning his ships, Cortés made sure the shoots of sugarcane that he had brought from Cuba had been unloaded at Veracruz.

Along the route to Jalapa (*Xalapa*), the travelers of the 19th century admired their first view of the country and tasted coffee. Once in the highlands, travelers should pay attention to the capitals of colonial silver: Zacatecas, with its alleyways and squares, a Baroque Guanajuato, and the winding Taxco, which adds to its tourist attractions the procession of hooded penitents during Lent.

Chile With Walnuts *(Mexico)* #8

INGREDIENTS
(Makes 4 servings)
1 pork sirloin
2 Tbsp. lard
1 tomato, finely chopped

2 cloves garlic, minced
1 onion
2 cups peeled almonds
⅓ cup seedless black
    raisins

8 *poblano* chiles
1 head of lettuce
1 pomegranate
2 hard-boiled eggs
2 cups walnuts

¾ cup cream
2 Tbsp. chopped
    parsley
Salt to taste

PREPARATION

Cube the sirloin, put it through the food processor and fry it in the lard for 30 minutes over medium heat together with the onion, garlic, chopped tomato, raisins, and peeled almonds. Add salt, allow the mixture to cool and set aside.

Roast the chiles in medium-hot oven for 35 minutes. Make a lengthwise incision in each of them, being careful not to break them so that they can be stuffed, and remove the seeds and membranes.

Stuff the chiles with the pork mixture and place them on a serving dish lined with lettuce leaves, covering them with the cream, slightly whipped.

Decorate with chopped parsley, walnut halves, hard-boiled egg slices and loose pomegranate grains. Serve cold.

> **TIP**
> To peel the almonds easily, dip them in boiling water, then rub them with a piece of cloth to take the skin off; let them dry and toast them in medium hot oven for 10 minutes before using them.

Mexican Rice (Mexico) #9

INGREDIENTS
(Makes 6 servings)

2 serrano chiles, seeds & membranes removed
2 onions
4 tomatoes
2 cloves garlic
6 oz. fresh sweet peas
6 Tbsp. olive oil
2 cups long grain rice
3 cups chicken broth
¼ tsp cumin
¼ tsp saffron
salt and pepper

PREPARATION

Using a food processor, chop the chiles along with the onions, tomatoes, garlic cloves and fresh, uncooked sweet peas. Set aside.

Heat the oil and fry the rice for 10 minutes over medium heat, stirring constantly with a wooden spoon so that it will cook evenly.

Slowly add the broth and continue stirring.

Add the vegetable mixture, mix and season with salt, pepper, cumin and saffron.

Cook over low heat, approximately 15 minutes, until the rice has absorbed the broth.

Turn off the heat. Cover the food with a dish towel, then cover the pot with its lid and let it rest for 5 minutes before serving.

> **NOTE**
> Frying the rice before cooking it will prevent it from becoming lumpy.

Metropolitan
Cathedral,
Mexico City.

In the north, interest in beef and goat stews grows. On the cattle-raising prairies, the regional barbecues and jerk beef dishes (*machacas* and *chilorios*) go well with guacamole and *frijolada ranchera*. Also typical of the north are the *menudos, birrias,* and sausages, the Mennonite cheeses from Cuauhtémoc, and beef barbecued Tampico-style, marinated in Seville orange juice.

In the deserts of Chihuahua prickly pears ripen, Indian fig jellies are made, and everyone drinks *tesgüino,* an indigenous corn spirit that accompanied solitary explorer Carl Lumholtz through Tarahumara country towards the end of the 19th century. The famous Chihuahua al Pacífico railroad crosses the Sierra Madre at the edge of the abyss; there are stops where tacos, empanadas, enchiladas, and barbecued dishes can be had, before it reaches the torrid plains of the Sea of Cortés.

Rice Poblano-Style *(Mexico)* #10

INGREDIENTS
(Makes 4 servings)
4 *poblano* chiles
½ cup olive oil
2 cups long grain rice

3 cups boiling chicken broth
1 onion, finely chopped
3 cloves garlic, crushed
kernels from 2 ears of corn
salt

PREPARATION

Roast two chiles for 5 minutes on high heat, peel them and remove the seeds and membranes. Cut them in thin strips and set aside for decoration. Grind up the remaining 2 chiles (without seeds or membranes) in a food processor, quickly sauté them in 2 Tbsp. oil for 5 minutes at high and set aside. Heat the remaining oil and fry the rice approximately 3 minutes at high until it becomes white, stirring constantly with a wooden spoon so that it will cook evenly. Gradually add the boiling broth and stir slowly but constantly.

Add the chopped onion, and the crushed garlic cloves, together with the corn kernels.

Cook approximately 20 minutes over medium heat; add the processed chiles at the end. Decorate with chile strips.

TIP
Instead of processed chiles, you can add a tsp of chili powder per cup of rice to increase flavor.

When Mexicans talk about the Pacific they refer above all to the coast between Mazatlán and Oaxaca. It includes the tourist paradises of Puerto Vallarta and Acapulco, which owes its first bout with fame to the American terminal of the mythical Manila Galleon, which carried spices and legends from the Orient to Mexico between 1571 and 1734. Shrimp, (broths, tacos, enchiladas, empanadas, tamales), barbecued fish, and cebiches rule on the coastal tables. On the beach visitors can sample the *botanas,* different types of fresh seafood prepared to order and served on *tostadas.*

Puebla had a fortunate childhood. The Spaniards founded it on the Royal road from Villa Rica de la Vera Cruz to Mexico and between two oceans, not far from the ships to Spain nor those to China. Not surprisingly, the best produce and recipes from abroad ended up in the cellars of the religious congregations of that culinary isthmus. Through Puebla de los Angeles there also passed peppers, tomatoes, and sweet potatoes. Even though it was never an Aztec town, Mexicans consider it the capital of

Avocado Soup (Mexico) #11

INGREDIENTS
(Makes 4 servings)
2 large avocados
2 cups chicken broth

¾ cup cream
2 Tbsp. chopped fresh
  coriander
6 flour or corn tortillas

1 Tbsp. lard
salt and pepper

PREPARATION

Heat the broth for 10 minutes over medium heat and add the cream to it. Peel the avocados, chop them in a food processor and add them to the broth, stirring constantly with a wooden spoon to mix the ingredients. Add salt and pepper.

Cut the tortillas in quarters and fry them in lard for 5 minutes over high heat.

Sprinkle the soup with chopped, fresh coriander and serve hot, together with the tortilla chips.

NOTE
Once the cream has been added to the broth, it is important not to let it reach boiling temperature at any time.

Bean Tamales (Mexico) #12

INGREDIENTS
(Makes 4 servings)
1 cup butter, softened
1 lb. rice flour

1 Tbsp. baking powder
20 corn husks
1 lb. black beans
1 bunch of *epazote* tea

or one leaf of *acuyo* or
avocado
1 small onion
1 clove garlic

¾ lb. soft cheese, sliced
into 20 slices
2 Tbsp. lard
salt

PREPARATION

Soak the beans at least four hours.

Beat the butter until creamy; add the rice flour, sifted with the baking powder, and continue beating as you blend in a little lukewarm water to form a solid dough.

Boil the beans in cold water with the onion, garlic, salt and *epazote* or the *acuyo* or avocado leaf until tender, about 30 minutes; drain them, take the vegetables out and fry the beans in lard until they are completely dry.

Stuff the corn husks with one Tbsp. of rice dough, one of beans and a slice of cheese. Form little packets that can be tied with strings made of husk. Cook them in a double boiler or a steamer for an hour.

---

patriotic gastronomy. It was in this city of churches and blue tiles that the nuns prepared the tricolor dish that symbolizes the national flag, using an appropriately whitish walnut sauce (*nogada*) to crown green chiles stuffed with ground beef and decorated with red pomegranate seeds. These walnut-covered chiles were tasted for the first time around 1821 and are considered even more Mexican when served on Talavera dishes from Puebla.

Even older and no less Creole is the mole from Puebla. This is a dish in which the *guajolote* — the Aztec turkey the Spanish chroniclers called the "dewlapped rooster" — is stewed and seasoned with a sauce of ground chiles, chocolate, and sesame seeds. Tradition has it that in the 17th century a certain convent cook happened to combine chiles and chocolate in her dreams, a mixture she then used to cook the turkey destined for a religious banquet. In fact, chocolate had long enhanced the flavor of chiles in Aztec cooking.

In pre-Hispanic Mexico, cocoa was a seed with nutritious, ritual, and

Photo: Carlos Mordo

Cape San Lucas, Southern Baja California, Mexico.

monetary value, and chocolate (*chocólatl*), a noble and divine beverage (ordinary folks drank atoles and pulques). According to Father Joseph de Acosta, "it is the prized drink, with which the Indians and the Spanish treat the gentlemen that come to their land or go through it; the Spanish women, used to the customs of the land, are especially fond of dark chocolate." It was drunk with atole, sweetened with honey, and perfumed with flower petals and aromatic herbs (milk chocolate had to wait until the end of the 19th century, and it is not American but Swiss). After the pagan gods had been silenced, chocolate was venerated in the cauldrons of the convents, spiced with cinnamon and anise and exported to Spain. Once the salubrious drink of the Aztec pantheon, chocolate became universally known as a human drink, available in the streets, markets, and hotels.

Stuffed Chiles (Mexico) #13

INGREDIENTS
(Makes 4 servings)
8 *poblano* chiles

salt
¾ lb. Cheddar cheese, cut
   into 8 equal slices

4 eggs, separated
1 cup flour
¾ cup olive oil

PREPARATION

Prepare chiles as described on page 9 and peel them. Make an incision on their sides, carefully removing the seeds and membranes, season them with salt and stuff them with some of the cheese. Beat the egg whites and the yolks separately, then add the yolks to the whites and blend them in softly until they are homogeneous. Add salt.

Coat the chiles with flour, dip them in the egg mixture, and fry them in oil for 5 minutes over high heat, taking care not to burn their surface. The oil must be hot but not boiling; as soon as the chiles start looking golden they should be removed from the oil and placed on paper towels to drain.

Serve with Mexican Rice (see Recipe #9).

> TIP
> Deep fry the chiles or baste them with hot oil to form a firm crust that will make it easier to turn them over.

Huevos Rancheros (Mexico) #14

INGREDIENTS
(Makes 2 servings)
4 flour or corn tortillas
   (Recipe #2)

2 Tbsp. oil
4 fried eggs
2 cups hot refried beans
   (Recipe #17)

SAUCE
2 *serrano* chiles
2 tomatoes, cubed
1 Tbsp. olive oil

salt and pepper
2 tsp. sugar

PREPARATION

SAUCE
Remove the seeds and membranes from the chiles, chop them and set them aside.

Put the cubed tomatoes through the food processor. Fry them in oil for 5 minutes at high until they thicken, add salt and pepper and a little sugar to take away their acidity. Remove from heat, add the chiles and allow to rest in the fridge for 6 hours. Serve hot.

TORTILLAS
Fry the tortillas in oil for 5 minutes at high; they may be soft or crunchy, according to your taste. Place on the plates, arranging a fried egg and a serving of hot refried beans on each, and cover with sauce.

Tinga Poblana (Mexico) #15

INGREDIENTS
(Makes 4 servings)
1 lb. flank steak or brisket
4 cups vegetable broth

2 *chipotle* chiles
1 clove garlic, crushed
2 tomatoes, cubed
1 onion, finely chopped

1 avocado
1 head of lettuce
3 Tbsp. lard
1 lemon

1 tsp. pepper
salt

PREPARATION

Cook the meat in the broth for one hour over medium heat; add salt and pepper. Let the meat cool in the broth; then take it out and break it up in very small pieces with two forks. Set aside.

Remove the seeds and white membranes from the chiles and chop them.

Fry the chopped onion in one Tbsp. of lard for 10 minutes over medium heat until transparent; add the crushed garlic, the tomatoes, the chiles and the beef. Add the remaining lard and cook for 10 minutes over medium heat, until the preparation thickens.

Serve on lettuce leaves, decorated with avocado slices.

NOTE
Do not forget to sprinkle the avocados with lemon juice to prevent discoloration.

Chicken Breasts with Walnuts *(Mexico)* #16

INGREDIENTS
(Makes 4 servings)
1 slice bread
4 Tbsp. milk
¼ lb. Toluca or any
  soft cheese

1 tsp. sugar
½ cup cream
½ cup sour cream
1 shot of sherry
1 cup walnuts, finely
  chopped

4 chicken breasts
salt and pepper

GARNISH
Seeds of 1 pomegranate
walnut halves

PREPARATION

Take the crust off the bread, soak it in milk, drain and set aside.

Melt the cheese in a thick-bottomed pan for 5 minutes over low heat so that it will not burn. Chop the walnuts using a food processor. Add the bread, sugar, cream, sour cream, sherry, and processed walnuts to the cheese and cook for about 10 minutes over medium heat, stirring constantly with a wooden spoon.

Add the breasts, salt and pepper and cook for 20 minutes over medium heat, turning the meat for even cooking.

Place the breasts on a serving dish together with the gravy, decorating with pomegranate seeds and walnut halves.

TIP
If you have no sour cream, use ½ cup regular cream with 1 Tbsp. lemon juice.

According to Aztec mythology, the first cocoa seeds were stolen by the god Quetzalcóatl and planted with the help of prayer. However, this fruit most likely traveled from Amazonia to the Aztec capital through Tabasco and Soconusco (Chiapas), hot lands where Mexico learned to drink chocolate. The territory becomes so narrow there that cebiches, shrimp broths, and fish barbecues are borrowed from one sea to the other. At the Gulf of Campeche they make barbecued or pickled needlefish with hot chiles and squash seeds. It is hard to go through Oaxaca without visiting Monte Albán — with the splendid ruins of a great indigenous ceremonial center — or tasting some of the seven *moles zapotecos*. The Mayan ruins of Otulum, better known by their Spanish name, Palenque, lie hidden between the forests of Chiapas and the savannahs of Yucatan.

Travelers expect to find fashionable beaches and monumental tourist archaeology (Chechén Itzá, Uxmal, and Tulum) in the Yucatan peninsula.

Refried Beans (Mexico) #17

INGREDIENTS
(Makes 4 servings)
2 cups beans
2 *jalapeño* chiles
2 onions
4 cloves garlic

3 quarts water
2 Tbsp. lard or vegetable oil
1 tomato, peeled, seeded,
  and chopped
Salt and pepper
coriander leaves

PREPARATION

Wash the beans thoroughly, changing the water several times. Drain and place the beans, the chiles, one of the onions and 2 cloves of garlic, crushed, in a pan with 3 quarts of water and simmer for one hour or until the beans start to shrivel. Add more hot water if necessary: the mixture should be moist but not liquid.

Halfway through the cooking time add a Tbsp. of lard or vegetable oil. Once cooked, season and set aside.

Finely chop the other onion and fry it in the remaining lard together with the chopped tomato and the remaining 2 cloves of garlic.

Mash four Tbsp. of the beans with part of the broth to form a thick paste and add them to the mixture. Cook for 30 minutes over medium heat until the mixture thickens.

Add this paste to the beans to thicken them and let them cool.

Drop the paste in 2-Tbsp. portions and fry them in lard for about 5 minutes over high heat; serve on a bed of coriander leaves.

NOTE
The bean paste must be thick and consistent to make frying easier. It is better to add salt to the beans at the end of the cooking time to prevent them from hardening.

Zacatecas,
Mexico.

The seafood cuisine — shrimp tacos, snail cebiche, codfish quesadillas —
is matched by the culinary offerings of the fruits of the earth: iguana stews,
suckling pig cooked in the Mayan fashion with Seville orange sauce, lime
soup with avocados, and *papadzules,* the regional crepes.

On the other end of the map, Baja California is the perpetual isthmus
that never becomes a peninsula. The ancients believed it was an island,
and tourists rarely prove them wrong, since they never go on firm land
unless they manage to take the Tijuana bus. At Baja there are organic
food cultivations, sei whale (*Balaenoptera borealis*) havens, Jesuit missions, and cave paintings. At Los Cabos there are extraordinary beaches
and luxurious hotels reminiscent of Hispanic Mexican architecture. At
mealtime, the traditional dishes come from the sea: ray tacos, chiles
stuffed with mollusks or lobster, lobster and beans, beans with fish, fish
with prickly pears. Clams are cooked under the sand with hot coals
(*almejadas*).

Tacos *(Mexico)* *#18*

INGREDIENTS
(Makes 6 servings)
1 large chicken breast
4 cups chicken broth
6 flour or corn tortillas

Olive or corn oil as
   needed
6 lettuce leaves

GUACAMOLE
2 avocados
1 onion
1 tomato
1 or 2 *poblano* chiles

2 Tbsp. chopped fresh
   coriander
juice of ½ lemon
2 Tbsp. vinegar
Salt

PREPARATION

Boil the chicken breast in the broth for 20 minutes over medium heat, cool and cut in thin strips. Mound the strips in the center of the tortillas and roll them. Heat the oil and fry the tacos for just a few seconds. Place them on a serving dish and serve with guacamole.

GUACAMOLE

Remove the seeds from the tomato and cube it; chop the onion coarsely. Remove the seeds and membranes from the chiles and cut them in small pieces without chopping them.

Break the avocados into small pieces with a fork and mash them coarsely, sprinkling them with lemon juice to prevent discoloration.

Mix all the ingredients. Season with salt, vinegar and coriander. Serve on lettuce leaves.

> **TIP**
> In order for the chicken breast to retain its natural color it must be left in the broth until the moment of using it.

Between the highlands and the sea, Jalisco has given Mexico three world symbols of Mexicanness: mariachis (who originally played music of cattle drivers and outcasts), *charrería* (rough cowboy boldness, stylized with time until it became sportive celebration) and, above all, tequila, used to prepare strong drinks, good to accompany tacos and crunchy chapulines. Tequila is rum made of maguey (the prickly agave or American century plant), which father Acosta calls *árbol de las maravillas* (wonder tree), and with which the ancient inhabitants made an alcoholic beverage that they called *octli* and the Spanish, *pulque*. At certain festivities, according to Friar Bernardino de Sahagún, "pulque was as abundant as water."

Before sugar cane changed the history, society, and confectionery of the Americas, the Aztecs made their sweets and sweetened their beverages with honey from the maguey and the fruit of the prickly pear (*nochtli*), the emblematic plant of Mexico. There are large prickly pear plantations in the center and north of the country, but the prickly pear always grew wild in the arid zone. Prickly pears play a part in the making of the hot Tlaxcaltecan *tlatlapas* and in the fervent Lent stews, with fish and squash. They are cooked stuffed with beans, in soups, stews and pickles. Prickly pears go well with cheese and sweets. The green, still sour prickly pear (*xoconostle*) is good for making sauces and coconut sweets.

Mexico's historical fruits are the avocado — which in the South American Andean region changes its Náhuatl name (*auacatl*) and takes on the

Cocadas *(Mexico)* *#19*

INGREDIENTS
(Makes 4 servings)
1 coconut
3 cups milk

1 cup sugar
4 egg yolks
1 cup whipping cream
butter as needed

PREPARATION

Take the coconut out of its shell and grate it. Set aside.

Place the milk and sugar in a saucepan and bring to a boil over low heat, stirring constantly to prevent sticking, until it thickens. Add the coconut to the milk in a fine shower without stopping the stirring motion, and cook over moderate heat for 20 minutes.

Stir the yolks without beating them and add them to the mixture, stirring over low heat with a whisk until it thickens, without letting it boil.

Allow the mixture to cool and pour into individual custard serving cups.

Chill for four hours. Pour melted butter on top of them and bake in pre-heated oven (350ºF) for 5 minutes until golden.

Cool and serve without removing from the cups, topped with lightly whipped cream.

> TIP
> To separate the coconut easily from its shell, heat it in a hot oven for a few minutes. Take it out and tap it several times with a hammer before breaking it.

Quechuan (*palta*) — *guanábanas, guayabas, chirimoyas, capulines* and the glorious *zapote* (*tzapotl*) or American medlar, which, in the words of Fernández de Oviedo, "has the best taste you can think of, and I have found nothing that can be compared to it."

Among the Mayas and Aztecs, the sacred and profane feasts reached both the altars and the kitchens. In the 16th century, Friar Diego de Landa tells that the natives of Yucatan buried their dead with their mouths stuffed with ground corn so that they would not go hungry in the afterlife. Even today, on All Souls' Day, the offerings of food are multiplied, and special dishes, such as *pan de muerto* (dead man's bread) and the popular *calabaza en tacha* (baked squash dessert), are prepared. The living cook for their dearly departed while the children play with sugar skulls.

A Creole table of the 19th century such as that of a well-to-do family who

Mexican Yemitas *(Mexico)* #20

INGREDIENTS
(Makes 4 servings)
10 egg yolks
2 cups sugar

½ cup milk
½ cup water
½ lemon
1 tsp. cinnamon powder

1 cinnamon stick
2 Tbsp. sweet liqueur

PREPARATION

Place the sugar in a saucepan, add the water, the lemon juice and the cinnamon stick and bring to a boil over very low heat without stirring until the syrup thickens, approximately 20 minutes. Take out the cinnamon stick and set aside.

Beat the egg yolks, milk and liqueur with a wire beater. Gradually add the warm syrup, mixing well, and cook over a diffusing disc, beating constantly, until the mixture breaks into a boil.

Remove from heat, cool and beat until creamy. Form small balls with your hands and coat them with sugar and cinnamon powder.

NOTE
Moisten your hands if necessary to prevent the mixture from sticking to them while making the balls.

could afford to entertain foreign travelers consisted of *puchero* with tortilla, stuffed chiles, barbecued beef with beans, sweets, fruit, coffee, and cigars. After an abundant breakfast, there is only one main meal, called precisely *la comida* (the meal), which is served at three o'clock in the afternoon. Wine and beer accompany the foods. *Champurrados* and *aguas frescas* (beverages made with blended fruits) are old drinks that have not lost their appeal. Mexicans produce good coffee at Oaxaca and Veracruz and enjoy it all over the country. Tamales are eaten with black coffee, hot chocolate, or atole.

At tourist enclaves and fashionable places, spices are used to accommodate the visitor's taste. The nouvelle cuisine explores the possibilities offered by the ancestral foods — prickly pears, avocados, huitlacoches, flowers, and aromatic herbs — applied to non-traditional culinary dishes such as salads, casseroles, crepes, and cebiches.

Photo: Panoramic Images

Parade Ground and Government Palace, Guadalajara, Mexico.

Recipe Glossary
(Mexico)

CHILES: hot peppers. There are over 200 varieties of chiles in Mexican cuisine. In general, the seeds and inner membranes of the chiles must be removed before using them to temper their flavor. It is advisable to wash your hands thoroughly after handling them, since they are a skin and eye irritant. Their degree of piquancy is measured in *scoville* units, the *habaneros* being the hottest.

WIDE CHILE: dark red, dry chile

CHIPLOTE CHILE: smoked chile, usually sold pickled.

JALAPEÑO CHILE: small, meaty fresh chile with a rounded end, about 5 to 10 inches long. It can be replaced by two *serrano* chiles. Very hot.

MULATTO CHILE: deep red dry chile, a relative of the dark *poblano*. Ideal for sauces, it is also served stuffed.

PASILLA CHILE: dark red, wrinkled dry chile. Highly aromatic and sweetly hot.

POBLANO CHILE: large fresh chile, milder than the smaller fresh chiles.

SERRANO CHILE: fresh chile, smaller than *jalapeño* and pointed. Very hot.

LARD: may be replaced by corn or olive oil.

MOLE: thick sauce made with chiles and spices.

NOGADA: walnut sauce.

OAXACA CHEESE: a typical cheese, may be replaced by mozzarella.

TOLUCA CHEESE: a typical cheese, may be replaced by soft cheese.

COCADAS: coconut candy or preserve.

YEMITAS: candied egg yolks.

CENTRAL AMERIC

A AND ANTILLES

Caribbean Sea   Photo: Panoramic Image

Some brought us water, others, things to eat; others, seeing that I made no attempt to go ashore, jumped into the sea and swam towards us and we understood they asked us whether we were come from the heavens. And an old one came in the small boat, and others clamored loudly, calling men and women: "Come and see the men who came from the heavens, bring them food and drink."

—Christopher Columbus

Central America is a land-bridge that joins two continents and lies between the two largest oceans of the world. During the 19th century this Spanish isthmus was split into six small nations that, reluctant to become one, divided it up along a mountain chain adjacent to the Pacific coast.

The indigenous people of Central America used cassava and corn as their bread, roasted their meat barbecue-style, salted their food with sea-water, celebrated with *chicha* and a smoke before going to sleep. Their everyday foods were part of their beliefs. The *Popol Vuh,* something akin to a Mayan Genesis, teaches that the creators of the world found in corn the primordial substance that gave life to man. According to the writer Fernández de Oviedo, the natives of Panama buried their workers with corn so that they might sow it in heaven.

Among the Central American nations, Guatemala has become a center of ethnographic, folkloric, and archaeological interest, thanks to its Mayan heritage. The Mayas had a variety of foods similar to that of the Aztecs and spread the culture of tortillas, peppers, frothy chocolate, atole (a refreshing drink made with corn flour, still popular at markets and novenas), mashed avocados, and prickly pear jellies. With the colonizers' introduction of cattle, bananas, sugar cane, and coffee, the natives' traditional food store was increased. The basic foods of the Central American countries remain corn, beans, and sorghum, produced mostly by subsistence farmers. Rice with speckled beans is a dish found everywhere.

Lack of industrialization keeps the barter economy and local food production alive, in turn contributing to the importance of the markets, still closely linked to the central plaza (the *tiangüiz* of pre-Columbian times) and the church. Street food vendors vie for the attention and appetites of potential clients with fried sliced plantains and pots of cassava or fish soups with vegetables, or even stews cooked on a bed of glowing coals.

Tical, Guatemala.

Ranchera Beans *(Guatemala)* #21

INGREDIENTS
(Makes 6 servings)
1 lb. black beans
½ cup butter

4 oz. *chicharrones* (see note)
½ cup grated semi-hard
   cheese
¾ cup whipping cream

2 tomatoes
2 onions
3 quarts water
salt

PREPARATION

Soak the beans in a quart of water for 12 hours. Drain and cook, covered, in two quarts of water for 4 hours over medium heat. Set aside.

Fry the chicharrones in butter for 20 minutes. Add the onions, finely chopped, the tomatoes, peeled, seeded and diced, and the beans, and continue cooking for 10 minutes. Remove from heat, add salt and the whipping cream at room temperature; stir well to mix all ingredients.

Serve in individual bowls and sprinkle with the grated cheese.

NOTE
Cut lard in small pieces and fry them in a frying pan, sprinkled with water; cook them until the water evaporates and the liquid fat separates from the crunchy chicharrones.

Chojín *(Guatemala)* #22

INGREDIENTS
(Makes 6 servings)
1 lb. pork tripe
2 onions
2 green peppers

juice of 2 sour oranges
1 bunch radishes
1 bunch mint leaves
1 quart water
salt

PREPARATION

Boil the pork tripe in one quart of water for 2 hours over medium heat. Set aside in the fridge.

Finely chop the onions, the radishes and the mint; add salt, sprinkle with the orange juice and set aside.

Finely chop the cold pork tripe, mix it with the onions, radishes and mint, and add the peppers, without seeds or membranes, finely chopped.

Serve cold.

> **NOTE**
> The oranges must be sour to lend the dish its authentic flavor.

Unlike the Spanish part of Central America, which reflects the food preferences of Andean and colonial origins, the Atlantic-facing slopes have a decidedly Afro-Caribbean influence. Bananas were the staple of blacks and mulattos on the coast. So long under foreign control, these nations were belittlingly nicknamed Banana Republics.

As seen on the map, the Antillean islands are neatly laid out from largest to smallest along an arc stretching from the tip of the Yucatan peninsula to the delta of the Orinoco. They provided the conquistadors' first encounters with the New World. Over the following four centuries four colonial empires extended their frontiers to include the Caribbean. The coveted islands changed hands through wars and piracy until they formed the most motley collection of island states in the world.

Sugar cane and tobacco became the backbone of Antillean economy. The sugar revolution went hand in hand with the importation of slaves for the plantations, thus determining the social and economic structure of the region. Old mansions and abandoned sugar mills are testimonies to the Caribbean scene between the 16th and 19th centuries.

Tamales de Rosicler *(Guatemala)* #23

INGREDIENTS
(Makes 6 servings)
2¼ lb. white corn on the cob
3 quarts water

⅓ cup lard
⅓ cup butter
1 cup milk
½ cup ricotta cheese
1 cup semi-hard cheese

1 lb. sugar
1 tsp. ground cinnamon
1 tsp. anise extract
1 tsp. *rosicler*
½ tsp. salt

tusa as needed
⅓ cup pitted prunes
½ cup peeled almonds
⅔ cup seedless white raisins

PREPARATION

Boil the corn in three quarts of water, covered, for 2 hours over medium heat, until the skin comes off. Remove the kernels, process them and place them in a bowl.

Add the lard, the butter, the milk at room temperature, the ricotta, the grated cheese, the sugar, the cinnamon, the anise extract, the rosicler cut in small pieces and the salt. Beat well with a wooden spoon until smooth.

Divide the mixture in six portions and place each in the center of a tusa; decorate with prunes, almonds and raisins and cover the filling with another tusa. Form into a packet, tie with thin strips of tusa and cook in a small amount of water for 15 minutes over medium heat.

Serve hot in its wrapping; only the filling should be eaten.

NOTE
Tusas are dried corn husks.

While searching for gold and putting his stomach to the test, Columbus tried cassava bread, which he found tasted not unlike chestnuts, unaware that the locals made it from the poisonous yucca. The natives appreciated the meat of iguanas and of agoutis, rodents as suited to the pot as the guinea pigs of Peru. They fished with bow and arrow and jerk-dried their meats or preserved them in peppers. Tastes have changed little since those natives first taught Europeans to smoke tobacco and sleep in hammocks. The diet of the Caribbean is based on rice, beans, meat, and fruit. The generous range of aromatic herbs is strongly present in kitchens. Coconut, sweet potatoes, and manioc are used for the islands' sweets, while puddings and exotic sauces benefit from the islands' vanilla, cinnamon, clove, and nutmeg production.

Guatemala, traditional textiles.

Yucca Cakes *(Guatemala)* #24

INGREDIENTS
(Makes 6 servings)
1 lb. yucca
2 Tbsp. butter

2 eggs
2 Tbsp. sugar
2 slices of white bread,
   crusts removed

1 tsp. ground
   cinnamon
1 Tbsp. honey
2 cups water

PREPARATION

Peel the yucca, cut it in small pieces, and boil it in half a quart of water for 30 minutes over medium heat. Remove, cool, drain and put through food processor.

Add the eggs, the sugar, the cinnamon and the bread, crumbled, and mix with a rubber spatula until all ingredients are well mixed.

Take small portions of the dough in your hands and form 1¾-inch cakes, about ¼-inch thick.

Fry them in butter for 5 minutes on each side over medium heat, until golden.

Pour honey over the warm cakes and serve.

TIP
The best yuccas are the heavier, smoother, milkier ones.

Ripe Banana Tamales (Costa Rica) #25

INGREDIENTS
(Makes 6 servings)
6 ripe bananas
2 Tbsp. wheat flour

1 Tbsp. butter
1 Tbsp. sugar
½ lb. soft cheese
1 tsp. allspice

1 tsp. ground cloves
4 cups water
banana leaves as needed
salt

PREPARATION

Boil the unpeeled bananas in a quart of water for 30 minutes over medium heat, until cooked. Remove, peel and run through food processor.

Mix the processed bananas with half of the soft cheese cut in small pieces. Add the butter, the flour, the sugar, the salt, the allspice and the ground cloves. Mix well to blend in all the ingredients.

Form tortillas about 3 inches in diameter and place a portion of soft cheese in the center of each. Fold the edges of the tortillas towards the center to make a square shape; wrap them in banana leaves forming a packet and tie with cotton twine.

Cook in boiling water in a double boiler for 20 minutes. Remove the twine and serve hot; eat only the filling.

Yucca Pudding (Costa Rica) #26

INGREDIENTS
(Makes 6 servings)
⅓ cup butter
1 cup sugar

4 eggs
2 lb. yucca, grated
1 cup grated semi-
    hard cheese

⅔ cup seedless black
    raisins
1 tsp. flour
1 tsp. baking powder

1 tsp. vanilla extract
½ tsp. salt
butter and flour as
    needed (for mold)

PREPARATION

Beat the butter at room temperature with the sugar until creamy.

Add, the salt, the eggs, one by one, the grated yucca, the baking powder and the flour, sifted together, the grated cheese, the raisins and the vanilla extract, stirring well after adding each ingredient. Mix well until smooth.

Grease and flour an 11-inch mold, pour the batter in and bake at medium (350ºF) for 40 minutes until golden.

Cool and serve.

Gallo Pinto con Barbudos *(Costa Rica) #27*

INGREDIENTS
(Makes 6 servings)
2½ cups black beans
1½ cups rice
2 onions
2 cloves garlic
2 sprigs thyme

2 Tbsp. lard
4 cups vegetable broth
6 cups water
salt

BARBUDOS
¾ lb. green beans
3 Tbsp. lard
2 Tbsp. flour
2 egg whites
2 egg yolks
salt

Wash the beans several times, taking out the dirt that floats in the water on the last rinse. Soak the beans in six cups of water for 30 or 40 minutes. Cook them in the soaking water, together with one whole onion, the cloves of garlic and the sprigs of thyme, covered, for 2 hours over medium heat, until the beans are tender.

Add the salt 10 minutes before the end of the cooking time. Drain and discard the onion, the garlic and the thyme. Set aside.

Boil the rice in the vegetable broth for 20 minutes over medium heat. Set aside.

Finely chop the remaining onion and sauté it in lard for 10 minutes over medium heat. Add the beans and salt, fry for 5 minutes and add the rice. Stir.

Serve with the barbudos.

BARBUDOS

Cook the green beans in water with salt for 40 minutes over medium heat, until tender. Drain thoroughly and set aside.

Beat the egg whites until they form stiff peaks; add the flour, the salt and the egg yolks, one at a time, blending in gently.

Dip the green beans in this batter and fry them for 5 minutes in very hot lard, a few at a time so that they do not stick to each other. They must be loose and crunchy.

PURIFIED LARD

It is important to purify the lard in order to fry the green beans uniformly. Once it is melted, skim the foam from its surface and separate the whey that forms in the bottom.

NOTE
It is important not to overcook the green beans since they will be fried later.

Photo:Gerard Sioen - Ag. Anzenberger

Curaçao,
Antilles.

Its beauty and cultural heritage have made the Caribbean a mecca for vacationers. The historic, geographical, and cultural backdrop common to the whole region has not erased its great diversity of native, colonial, and African influences. France, England, and Holland vied for the islands but did not do as much for the cuisine as the African slaves, Bengali braziers, and Javanese and Chinese coolies brought over to replace the blacks freed at the end of slavery in 1840.

African vitality survives in religious observances. In the Caribbean, Christian saints may be venerated through traditional African rites, such as in Haiti's voodoo, associated with beating drums, magic, and ritual food and drink. Afro-Cuban saint-worship is practiced at family altars where offerings of

Meat Pies *(Honduras)* #28

INGREDIENTS
(Makes 12)

DOUGH

3 cups wheat flour
2 Tbsp. cooking oil
1 Tbsp. club soda
1 tsp. achiote

1 cup lukewarm water
1 tsp. salt
1 tsp. pepper

FILLING

1 lb. ground pork
2 tomatoes, peeled,
  seeded and diced
2 potatoes
1 onion, finely chopped
1 sweet pepper,
  seeded and chopped
4 cloves garlic, crushed
4 Tbsp. lard

1 cup sweet wine
1 Tbsp. vinegar
1 tsp. achiote
2 cups water
salt and pepper
cooking oil as needed

PREPARATION

DOUGH

Mix the flour with a tsp. of achiote, the salt and the pepper; pour out on flat surface, form a well and place the soda water, the oil and the lukewarm water in its center. Mix until you get a smooth, firm dough. Cover it with a cheesecloth and let it rest for 20 minutes. Set aside.

FILLING

Mix the ground pork with the vinegar. Add the diced tomatoes, the chopped onion, one tsp. of achiote; the crushed garlic and the pepper, without seeds or membranes and chopped, and fry everything in lard for 20 minutes over medium heat. Add salt and pepper and set aside.

Peel the potatoes and boil them in 2 cups of water for 30 minutes over medium heat. Remove, cube and add to the mixture, together with the sweet wine. Chill in the fridge for an hour.

ASSEMBLY

Roll the dough with a rolling pin to a thickness of ⅛-inch and cut 4-inch-diameter discs. In the center of each place two Tbsp. of the filling and moisten the edges with water at room temperature.

Fold each disc in half and press the edges firmly with your fingers to keep the filling in.

Fry in very hot oil until golden. Serve with chopped cabbage salad.

> **Note**
> You can press the edges of the meat pies with the tines of a fork.

Quesadillas *(Honduras)* *#29*

INGREDIENTS
(Makes 4 servings)
1⅓ cups rice flour
¾ cup sugar
1 cup semi-hard cheese

½ cup ricotta cheese
3 egg yolks
3 egg whites
2 Tbsp. butter
2 tsp. baking powder

butter as needed (for the molds)
flour as needed (for the molds)
salt

PREPARATION

Grate the cheese and mix it with the ricotta, the butter at room temperature and the sugar.

Add the egg yolks, one at a time, mixing after each until all ingredients are well mixed; add the rice flour and the baking powder, sifted together. Mix.

Beat the egg whites until they form stiff peaks and add them to the mixture blending in gently, with upward movements, until smooth.

Place in individual molds, greased and floured, and bake at 350°F for 15 minutes. Serve hot. They may be topped with strawberry sauce blended with liqueur and orange juice.

Banana Pudding (Honduras) #30

INGREDIENTS
(Makes 6 servings)
6 bananas
¾ cup. whipping cream

3 cups sugar
2 tsp. vanilla extract
3 eggs
2 cups water

½ Tbsp. butter and flour
  (for the mold)
6 egg whites

PREPARATION

Boil the bananas in their skins in 2 cups of water for 30 minutes over medium heat. Remove, peel and run through food processor.

Add the whipping cream, half of the sugar, the vanilla extract and the eggs and mix all ingredients well with a rubber spatula.

Grease and flour a pudding mold, pour the mixture into it and bake at 350ºF for 45 minutes. Remove.

Beat the egg whites with the remaining sugar for 20 minutes, until they reach meringue consistency. Cover the pudding and place in 350ºF oven for 15 minutes, allowing the meringue to cook without browning.

Remove and serve cold.

Chimano Hen *(Nicaragua)* *#31*

INGREDIENTS
(Makes 8 servings)
1 4.5-lb. stewing hen
salt and pepper
4 Tbsp. cooking oil
4 cups water

1 carrot, thinly sliced
2 bay leaves
1 tsp. nutmeg
1 zucchini, cubed
2 Tbsp. seedless white
    raisins

2 Tbsp. lard
2 Tbsp. wheat flour
1 cup sweet wine
2 Tbsp. sugar
2 Tbsp. Worcestershire
    sauce

4 white potatoes,
    peeled and quartered
2 Tbsp. capers
1 tsp. crushed red
    pepper

Photo: Florencia Podestá

Beach in
Costa Rica.

PREPARATION

Cut the hen in 8 pieces and sprinkle salt and pepper over them. Fry them in oil for 5 minutes on each side over medium heat.

Place the pieces in a pot and add 4 cups of water, the sliced carrot, the bay leaves and the nutmeg. Cover and cook for 30 minutes over medium heat, until the meat is tender.

Add the cubed zucchini and the raisins. Continue cooking until the zucchini is tender.

Melt the lard in a frying pan, add the flour, mix and cook for 5 minutes over medium heat, until the flour is toasted. Add it to the mixture; add the wine, the sugar, the Worcestershire sauce, the quartered potatoes, the capers and the crushed red pepper. Cook for 20 minutes over medium heat.

Serve hot in individual bowls.

arums, gumbo, mashed yams, and other foods of African origin have survived slavery. Trinidad's calypso originated on the plantations where slaves were induced to increase production by singing while they worked. Similarly, Trinidad's carnival may be a relic of old African festal entertainments.

In Jamaica, Rastafarians created a peaceful movement to show their disdain for the injustices perpetrated by whites. Their followers enthroned the Emperor of Ethiopia as a god, even though Ethiopians were never brought as slaves to the Caribbean. "Rastas" give great importance to their cooking, which is basically vegetarian, seasoned with peanuts, coconut milk, pepper, garlic, and fruit juices.

Steamed Meat (Nicaragua) #32

INGREDIENTS
(Makes 6 servings)
2¼ lb. stewing beef,
   cubed
salt and pepper
banana leaves as
   needed

6 cups water
2 green bananas,
   peeled
2 ripe bananas,
   unpeeled
1 lb. yucca
6 sausages

SAUCE
1 onion
1 hot red pepper
1 tomato
2 Tbsp. vinegar
4 Tbsp. water
juice of 1 sour orange

salt and pepper

GARNISH
1½ cups rice
4 cups vegetable broth
salt

PREPARATION

Cube the meat, add salt and pepper and distribute it over the banana leaves, previously washed. Close the leaves forming packets and marinate in the fridge for 24 hours.

Place a steamer in a thick-bottomed pot and add the water, making sure the level does not rise above the bottom of the steamer.

Cover the steamer with banana leaves, and then place the peeled green bananas, the unpeeled ripe bananas and the meat packets on the leaves. Place the yucca, peeled, cubed and sprinkled with salt, over the other ingredients, and cover with banana leaves.

Cover the pot and steam for 2 to 3 hours over medium heat, until the meat and the yucca are tender.

Wash the sausages, add them to the pot and continue cooking, covered, for 45 minutes.

Serve in individual bowls. Garnish with rice. Serve the sauce separately for guests to help themselves.

SAUCE

Finely chop the onion and the pepper, without seeds or membranes, and cube the tomato, peeled and seeded. Mix them in a bowl, add the vinegar, the water and the orange juice. Add salt and pepper, mix well and serve in a sauce boat.

GARNISH

Boil the rice in the broth for 20 minutes over medium heat. Add salt to taste.

> **NOTE**
> It is important to keep the proper level of water throughout the steaming process in order to ensure even cooking of all the ingredients.

Trinidad and Tobago are good examples of the influence of four continents converging on islands. The island of Trinidad is presented as a microcosm of language, feasts, divinities, and dress. They say that *calalu* (an African stew equivalent to the Brazilian *caruru*) is symbolic of the great ethnic mix of the country where some dozen countries' cooking is offered, including Spanish-American. Hindus and Muslims from India brought mango chutneys, curries, and *roti*, a Trinidadian version of the Indo-Pakistani *chapatti*. Descendants of Asians diversified their use of rice, considered the great popular dish of the Antilles.

Trinidad also played an important role in the history of chocolate. One of the three botanical species of cocoa is native to the island and was cultivated there by European colonists and taken to other continents. Jamaica on the other hand is a coffee producer. The natives called that island

Patacones Soup *(Panama)* #33

INGREDIENTS
(Makes 6 servings)

PATACONES

3 green bananas

2 Tbsp. corn oil

SOUP

1½ cups lentils

8 cups water

2 tomatoes, peeled,
  seeded and diced

1 onion, finely chopped

2 cloves garlic, crushed

salt

PREPARATION

PATACONES

Peel the bananas, cut them in 1-inch slices and fry them in the hot oil for one minute. Remove, flatten the slices with a rolling pin until paper thin, and fry them again for another minute, until golden. Set aside.

SOUP

Soak the lentils for 12 hours in a 4 cups of the water. Drain and boil them in the remaining 4 cups of water for an hour over medium heat, together with the tomatoes, peeled, seeded and diced, the onion, finely chopped, and the crushed garlic. Add salt at the end of the cooking period.

Drain and set the broth aside. Process all the ingredients, mix them with the patacones and cook them in the reserved broth for 5 minutes.

Serve hot in individual bowls.

Carimañolas (Panama) #34

INGREDIENTS (Makes 6 servings)	1 egg yolk	1 onion	4 Tbsp. tomato purée
2¼ lb. manioc	FILLING	1 green pepper, seeded	salt and pepper
4 cups water	1 lb. lean pork	1 clove garlic	olive oil
salt	olive oil as needed	1 tomato, peeled and seeded	

PREPARATION

Peel the manioc, cut it in medium-sized pieces and boil it in a quart of water with one Tbsp. of salt for 30 minutes over medium heat, until tender. Remove, drain and process hot.

Before the manioc cools, add the egg yolk, mix well, take small portions of the mixture and form 1¼-inch balls. Set aside.

FILLING

Cut the pork in small pieces and fry it in the oil for 5 minutes over medium heat. Remove, allow to cool and run it through food processor with the onion, the green pepper, without seeds or membranes, the clove of garlic and the tomato. Add the tomato purée, add salt and pepper and cook, covered, for 15 minutes over medium heat. Remove and cool in the fridge for 30 minutes.

Press the manioc balls in the center to make them hollow, stuff them with the filling and cover the indentation with moistened hands. Taper the ends and fry them in the very hot oil for 5 minutes on each side until golden. Serve hot.

Oil Dong with Dumplings (Grenada) #35

INGREDIENTS
(Makes 4 servings)

OIL DONG
1 lb. salt fish
2 whole coconuts
2 tsp. ground turmeric
4 cups water
8 Tbsp. vegetable oil
1 lb. chicken wings
1 lb. pig tail
4 green bananas, peeled & quartered
4 onions, finely chopped
4 cloves garlic, finely chopped
4 sprigs chive, chopped
4 sprigs parsley, chopped
4 leaves sweet basil, chopped
4 leaves fresh mint, chopped
4 leaves oregano, chopped
4 leaves coriander, chopped
2 bird peppers
2 green peppers
1 breadfruit, peeled & quartered
salt and pepper

DUMPLINGS
4 cups flour
½ cup butter, melted
1 tsp. cinnamon
1 tsp. salt
water as needed

PREPARATION

OIL DONG
Soak the salt fish in water for 8 hours. Remove and set aside.

Cut the coconuts, remove their pulp and grate it finely. Place it in a pot and mix it with the turmeric and 4 cups of boiling water. Pour everything into a cheesecloth bag to extract the coconut milk. Set aside.

Place the oil in a thick-bottomed pot and heat for 5 minutes at high; add the chicken wings and fry them for 5 minutes on each side, until golden.

Add the coconut milk, the pig tail, the salt fish, the green banana quarters, the chopped onions and garlic, the chives, the parsley, the basil, the mint, the oregano and the coriander. Add the whole bird peppers, the green peppers — without seeds or membranes, cut in thin strips — and the breadfruit quarters. Add salt and pepper and cook, covered, for 20 minutes over medium heat. Add the dumplings, cover and continue cooking for 20 minutes, until the pig tail and the salt fish are done. Stir once in a while with a wooden spoon to prevent the food from sticking to the bottom of the pot.

Serve hot in individual bowls.

DUMPLINGS
Place the flour, the melted butter, the cinnamon, and the salt in a bowl and mix all ingredients well. Gradually add the water and mix with your hands until soft and smooth but firm.

Take small portions of the dough and form 2-inch-long cylinders.

NOTE
In order for the oil dong to cook evenly, the ingredients must be always covered by the coconut milk. Should it be necessary, add dairy milk.

Photo: Carlos Mordo

San Blas,
Panama.

Xaymaca, the land of forest and water. It is also the land of beaches that attract thousands of tourists, of fishing villages, and of green ranges of mountains where the famous Blue Mountain coffee grows.

Pork is the main staple of Caribbean cooking. It was brought from Iberian piggeries to the tables of the Antilles with all the honors due to festival dishes. This was made possible by buccaneer cookery. The first buccaneers (*boucaniers*) were rustic Frenchmen who hunted sea turtles and wild pigs. They roasted their meat on the barbecue (*boucan*) following old native customs and sold their jerk-dried meat (*viande boucanée*) to passing ships and pirates. When they were expelled from Española (Columbus's favorite island) they moved to the Tortugas. In changing from dried meats to rum and firearms they were able to recruit others and convert to piracy.

Rice and Peas *(Jamaica)* #36

INGREDIENTS
(Makes 3–4 servings)
¾ cup kidney beans
7 cups water
black pepper as needed
1 green onion, finely

chopped
1 clove garlic, finely
chopped
1 sprig of thyme, finely
chopped
2 cups coconut milk

1½ tsp. salt
2½ cups white rice

Wash the beans in a strainer until the water runs clear. Soak them in 2 cups of the water for four hours and drain.

Boil the beans in 5 cups of water with a dash of black pepper for half an hour over medium heat, until they start to get tender, adding the salt halfway through the cooking time and more water if necessary. Add the chopped green onion, garlic and thyme. Bring the heat to low and simmer for about 30 minutes until the beans are tender without becoming mushy. Drain and set aside both the beans and the cooking broth.

Add enough cooking broth to the coconut milk to complete a quart of liquid, adding water if necessary. Place the liquid in a pot, add salt to taste, another dash of pepper and simmer until it breaks into a boil. Add the rice, cover and cook for 10 minutes. Add the beans, cover and continue cooking for another 10 minutes, until the rice is done.

Serve very hot as a garnish for chicken sautéed in a pot with abundant green onion and garlic. Serve the juices of the chicken over the rice.

> **NOTE**
> To prepare the coconut milk, cut the coconut pulp in small pieces and put them through the blender with 3 cups of water; strain to separate the pulp from the milk.

A similar case was that of Jamaica's Maroons. These fiercely independent blacks from Guinea escaped from the plantations and formed runaway communities that resisted the colonial powers. They hunted wild boar, roasted them well spiced on underground barbecues and sold the dried jerky. As this became famous, the pork came out of the jungle to the tables of the English governor and sugar barons and set a precedent for a national form of cooking still found in the spicy meats cooked over wood fires.

Jean Baptiste Labat (Le Père Labat), a voracious Dominican priest and expert on buccaneer and fugitive slave cooking, roamed the beaches where turtles and wild boar were smoked, and religiously wrote down the recipes, to become a devotee of *cochon marron* and stewed turtle or turtle paté.

Fruit is used in the preparation of cooling drinks, ice creams, punch, and sweets, and also for sauces and chutneys. Sea bass and other fish are roasted in the oven with tropical fruits. Pawpaws (papayas) are used in gratins and stews and stuffed with meats. Jamaican garden fruits are grilled. As in all tropical American countries plantains are considered fruit, vegetable, bread, or sweets, depending on the role they play at mealtime.

Mangos, cashews, and breadfruit were all introduced to the Antilles as cheap food for slaves. Breadfruit is native to islands in the Pacific where Captain James Cook discovered it prevented scurvy. Another great sailor, Captain William Bligh, planted it on St. Vincent. Breadfruit is eaten oven-roasted, fried like potatoes, or stuffed with minced meat or fish. In Barbados it is preferred boiled with a covering of sauce. In Martinique roast suckling pig is accompanied by breadfruit fritters. On St. Vincent and Granada it is the indispensable ingredient of oil dong, a stew that is eaten out of doors with friends.

Palmitos Fruit Salad *(Dominican Republic)* #37

INGREDIENTS
(Makes 6 servings)
1 head of lettuce
1 melon, peeled & cubed
6 carambolas, peeled & thinly sliced
1 apple, peeled & diced
3 Tbsp. orange juice
1 can hearts of palms
3 Tbsp. lemon juice
3 Tbsp. honey
1 tsp. ground mustard
3 Tbsp. mango chutney
3 Tbsp. olive oil
salt and pepper

CHUTNEY
2 onions, finely chopped
1 green pepper, seeded & finely chopped
1 red pepper, seeded & finely chopped
2 mangos, peeled & chopped
7 oz. light brown sugar
1 Tbsp. rock salt
1½ Tbsp. mustard seeds
4 cups cider vinegar

PREPARATION

Wash the leaves of lettuce, dry them, spread them on a serving dish and distribute the cubed melon, carambolas and apple on them. Sprinkle with the orange juice and set aside.

Wash the hearts of palms, cut them in 1½-inch pieces and spread them over the fruit.

Mix the lemon juice, the honey, the mustard and the chutney. Beat them with an electric beater for 5 minutes, to mix the ingredients well. Gradually add the olive oil and continue beating at low, until the sauce thickens.

Add salt and pepper, pass through a sieve and pour over the fruit salad.

Chill for one hour.

Serve cold.

CHUTNEY

Mix chopped onions and peppers with the peeled, chopped mangos, the light brown sugar, the rock salt and the mustard seeds.

Place all the above ingredients in a stainless steel pot, add six Tbsp. of the vinegar and cook for 10 minutes over medium heat.

Gradually add the remaining vinegar and cook for 45 minutes until the mixture thickens.

Lechada Roja (Virgin Islands) #38

INGREDIENTS
(Makes 6 servings)
1¼ lb. guavas
2½ cups water

2 oz. tapioca grains
1⅓ cup. sugar
⅓ cup seedless white
  raisins

⅓ cup seedless black
  raisins
1 tsp. ground cinnamon
1 pinch nutmeg

1 pinch mace
1 pinch salt
1 tsp. vanilla extract
1 tsp. red food coloring

PREPARATION

Peel the guavas, seed them, cut them in small pieces and cook them in 2 cups of water for 20 minutes over medium heat. Drain and set aside.

In the remaining water, cook the tapioca with the sugar, the raisins, the spices and the salt for 20 minutes, until the grains of tapioca are tender.

Remove from heat, add the vanilla extract and the red food coloring and mix.

Pour the mixture in individual molds and distribute the guavas over them. Chill, unmold and serve.

> **NOTE**
> For easier unmolding, moisten the molds with water before pouring in the mixture.

When the landlord stopped importing foodstuffs slaves were allowed to cultivate their own vegetable patches and to sell the surplus on Sundays, their only free day. This is the origin of the Antillean weekly markets, which offer a great variety of fresh produce and local spices. While in the bars rum is drunk accompanied by fried fish tidbits, in the rowdy kitchens seafood turnovers, dumplings, chicken fritters, and supposedly aphrodisiac soups are prepared. Haitian markets and food are common subjects in the colorful national paintings.

As for drink, rum is the Antillean contribution to the world. In Caribbean nations it represents the third traditional source of foreign currency after sugar and bananas. This sugar cane brandy is drunk in bars, distilled in traditional ways in old distilleries, which welcome visitors. Each island has its own homemade liquors and punch. The national cool drinks sold on the streets are fruit juices, coconut milk, and *guarapo* — iced freshly sqeezed sugar cane juice.

Recipe Glossary (Central America and Antilles)

COSTA RICA

LARD: may be replaced by corn or olive oil.
PLÁTANO: plantain.
YUCA: yucca, manioc.

GUATEMALA

CHICHARRONES: the small, crunchy pieces left after melting lard.
LARD: may be replaced by corn or olive oil.
ROSICLER: a red Guatemalan plant with a light pink fruit.)
TUSA: dried corn husk.
YUCA: yucca, manioc.
CHOJÍN: chojin, a dish with ground meat and turnips.

HONDURAS

ACHIOTE: achiote seeds, may be replaced by saffron.
CHILE: pepper
PLÁTANO: plantain.

VIRGIN ISLANDS

GUAVA: the green or yellow fruit of the guava tree. Its pulp is pink or yellowish green, with a sour, refreshing taste.
MACIS: mace — bright red cover of the nutmeg.
TAPIOCA: manioc starch.

NICARAGUA

LARD: may be replaced by corn or olive oil.
PLÁTANO: plantain.
YUCA: yucca, manioc.

PANAMA

PATACÓN: plantain sliced thin and fried.

DOMINICAN REPUBLIC

CARAMBOLA: gold-colored fruit, sweet with a slightly acid taste.

CUBA AND PUERTO RICO

Cuba was the last of Spain's colonies in tropical America. She is Spanish-American and mulatto, made up of descendants of Spanish colonists, African slaves, and indentured Chinese. The Taino natives of Cuba and Puerto Rico did not survive colonial economies. Their legacy is cassava bread and yams, sweet potatoes and the fruits that now accompany meat and rice dishes. Some native barbecuing techniques are still applied today to pork and other Spanish meats.

When Columbus first discovered the wonders of the Caribbean, Cuba was not known to be an island nor American. When these virgin lands were incorporated into the map, Columbus himself recommended to the Spanish crown the introduction of cattle for meat. Even before sugar and tobacco Cuba produced and sold *tasajo* (dried meat) to passing ships. This first experiment with cattle gave rise to a taste for slow-cooked and basted meat: jerked beef with cassava or beans, and *ropa vieja* ("old clothes") — boiled meat, shredded, with tomato sauce.

Cubans love roast pig and rice with chicken or fried eggs. Colored and spiced rice is a main dish; white rice is an accessory. Rice with black beans is called "Moors and Christians" (*Moros y Cristianos*). Rice with red beans is *Congri*. Seafood is mostly for tourists, but long before lobster and shrimp were offered on the beaches of Varadero, slaves and native-born Spaniards were eating dried cod with yams and tomatoes and fried or stewed braize.

Cuban Spanish cooking favors thick soups of meat with vegetables and beans. Broths are made from meat on the bone, chicken, or fish heads. When root vegetables (*viandas*), rice, or potatoes are added they become soups. *Ajiaco,* the king of soups, is served as a main course. This Cuban dish is prepared with ingredients of several origins — Spanish (chicken, pork, garlic), African (arum, plantains), and native (cassava, sweet potatoes, yams) — but has a flavor all its own.

All Cuban meals have something fried, from chicken and fish to sweet potatoes or cassava. Cuban ropa vieja is served with fried bread. Plantain,

View of Havana
from Fort
La Cabaña.
Cuba.

Chicken Chilindron *(Cuba) #39*

INGREDIENTS
(Makes 6 servings)
1 4½-lb. chicken
salt
1 tsp. pepper

2 Tbsp. flour
6 Tbsp. vegetable oil
¼ lb. bacon
½ cup rum
2 cloves garlic, crushed

1 Tbsp. sugar
1 cup red wine
2 cups water
1 Tbsp. chopped parsley

Cut the chicken in 8 pieces, add salt and pepper and coat with flour. Fry the pieces in five Tbsp. of oil for 10 minutes on each side over medium heat, until golden. Drain and set aside.

Dice the bacon and sauté it in an ungreased pan for 5 minutes over medium heat. Drain and set aside.

In an ungreased pan, place a Tbsp. of oil, place the pieces of chicken and flambé them with the rum. Add the crushed cloves of garlic, the bacon and the sugar and heat, constantly turning the pieces of chicken to coat them with caramel.

Add the wine, allow the liquid to reduce for 3 minutes, until the alcohol evaporates, and set aside.

Place the pieces of chicken in a casserole dish, add the half quart of water and bake for 20 minutes at medium, until tender.

Remove, sprinkle with chopped parsley and serve hot with Creole sauce (see recipe N° 48).

> **NOTE**
> For the flambé, pour the rum on the pieces of chicken, light it, and allow the flame to die down as the alcohol evaporates.

---

fried and thinly sliced (*mariquitas*), is enjoyed as an appetizer in lieu of french fries; potatoes reached Cuba late and are not as popular as on the American continent. Fried plantains thickly sliced, on the other hand, are the accompaniment for roast meat. Another national fried food is pork-fat chitterlings, which are good with Moors and Christians and appreciated between sips of rum. Slaves mashed plantains and chitterlings together to make *fufu,* which they ate as a mash or in fufu balls.

African Cuba expresses itself principally in *calalú,* a dish of boiled meat and vegetables with tender arum leaves and all the root vegetables the country has to offer — yams, sweet potatoes, cassava, even squash and okra. When the slaves were allowed to breed, eat, and sell their own pigs the native tamales were enhanced by the addition of bits of pork to the corn. Pork ribs rather than dried meats were added to the stewed meat and vegetables, though the traditional fried plantains were never abandoned. Okra is equivalent to Brazilian *quiabo,* offered, together with arum, fufu, and peanuts, at family altars.

Plantation prosperity and privilege turned Havana into the rich and elegant capital city of Spanish America. Impressed by the abundance of

Caribbean Red Snapper (Cuba) #40

INGREDIENTS
(Makes 4 servings)
8 red snapper, red
   porgy or sea bass
   fillets
salt and pepper
4 Tbsp. lemon juice

½ lb. shrimp
1½ cups water
1 Tbsp. vinegar
1 tsp. peppercorns
1 cup dry white wine
2 bay leaves
2 Tbsp. vegetable oil

4 Tbsp. white sauce
½ lb. semi-hard cheese

WHITE SAUCE
¼ cup butter
2 Tbsp. flour
2 cups milk, heated

salt and pepper
½ tsp. nutmeg

GARNISH
4 boiled white
   potatoes

PREPARATION

Sprinkle the fish fillets with salt, pepper and lemon juice and marinate in the fridge for an hour.

Place the cleaned shrimp in a bowl, add 1½ cups of water, the vinegar, the peppercorns, the wine and the bay leaves and cook for 5 minutes over medium heat. Drain, set the cooking liquid aside, let the shrimp cool and chop them finely.

Brush an oven pan with the oil, place four fillets on it and cover each of them with a portion of shrimp.

Cover with the remaining fillets, pour the cooking liquid in the pan and cover it with aluminum foil. Cook for 10 minutes at 350ºF. Remove and drain the liquid.

Place one Tbsp. of white sauce on each fillet, cover with grated cheese and put back in the hot oven at 400ºF for 5 minutes, until golden.

Remove and serve hot. Garnish with boiled potatoes.

WHITE SAUCE
Melt the butter over medium heat. Remove from heat and add the flour, mixing well with a wooden spoon. Add the hot milk, stirring constantly, and cook for 10 minutes over medium heat until the sauce thickens. Add salt, pepper and nutmeg.

Pork with Papaya (Cuba) #41

INGREDIENTS
(Makes 6 servings)
2 red peppers
3 lb. pork loin
salt
1 tsp. ground pepper
1 onion, finely chopped
2 cloves garlic, crushed

2 Tbsp. sugar
1 cup red wine
1 tsp. flour
4 Tbsp. canned
    pineapple juice
1 cup water
2 green papayas, peeled
    & diced

4 Tbsp. vegetable oil

GARNISH
3 white potatoes
3 sweet potatoes
2 cups vegetable broth
2 Tbsp. chopped parsley

PREPARATION

Roast the peppers for 15 minutes at high. Peel them, remove the seeds and membranes and cut in thin strips. Set aside.

Dice the meat and add salt and pepper. Heat the oil in a dutch oven and fry the meat for 5 minutes at high. Add the chopped onion and the crushed cloves of garlic and fry for another 5 minutes. Immediately add the sugar and the wine to coat the meat with caramel, and allow the liquid to reduce for 5 minutes. Sprinkle the concoction with the wheat flour and mix well to distribute it uniformly, add the pineapple juice and the water, and simmer, covered, for 20 minutes.

Add the peppers and the diced papaya, and continue cooking for 10 minutes.

Serve hot in individual bowls.

Garnish with the potatoes and sweet potatoes, boiled in broth for 25 minutes, quartered and sprinkled with chopped parsley.

NOTE
Papaya is an excellent natural source of vitamins A, B1, B2, B5, E, C and minerals.

Moros y Cristianos *(Cuba)* #42

INGREDIENTS

(Makes 6 servings)

1½ cups black beans

2 quarts water

1 sprig of thyme

1 green pepper, seeded &
finely chopped

¾ lb. lean pork, cubed

4 Tbsp. corn or sunflower
oil

2 onions, finely chopped

2 cloves garlic, crushed

¼ tsp. cayenne pepper (not
ground)

3 cups rice

salt

1 tsp. black pepper

Wash the beans in abundant water. Place them in a thick-bottomed pot with 8 cups of water, the thyme and half the chopped green pepper.

Cook for 20 minutes at high, until it starts boiling; turn heat to low and simmer for 3 hours, covered, until the beans are tender. Add hot water if necessary.

Drain and set the cooking broth aside. Remove one Tbsp. of beans and mash them until smooth. Set aside.

Heat oil until very hot and fry cubed pork for 10 minutes, until it browns. Remove the meat, dry with paper towels and set aside.

In the same oil sauté the remaining chopped green pepper and onions, the crushed garlic, and the cayenne pepper, for 5 minutes over medium heat. Add the mashed beans, the rest of the beans and the pork and cook for another 10 minutes, uncovered.

Pour the mixture into a pot, add the reserved broth, the rice, add salt and pepper and cook for 30 minutes over medium heat until the liquid evaporates and the rice is done.

Serve hot in individual bowls.

> **NOTE**
> The beans should be washed until the water comes out clear.

monuments and colorful houses, visitors describe the Cuban capital as one of the most animated and happy cities of the Americas. In the 19th century, during the belle époque of sugar, travelers attended social gatherings in formal attire. An invitation to a good meal was one way to gain entry to society. At that time Cuban tables competed with the best in Europe in the variety and perfection of the dishes served.

The beach had not yet become an attraction, so travelers visited sugar plantations and mills, coffee plantations and tobacco growers, and saw how the slaves lived. There they found the mash dishes invented by slaves. In the slave-states of America, blacks mashed the same squashes, plantains, and vegetables that the Europeans preferred whole in their stews. At the same time a lasting mix was evolving in the kitchens. In many households shopping and the selection of menus were left to the African cooks, and these transferred their own taste to the white man's table; thus were flavors interwoven.

Rice Cuban Style (Cuba) #43

INGREDIENTS
(Makes 6 servings)

½ lb. bacon, diced

1 lb. baked ham, sliced thick & diced

2 Tbsp. butter

2 onions, finely chopped

1 green pepper, seeded & finely chopped

1 clove garlic, crushed

3 cups rice

1 tomato, peeled, seeded & diced

2 Tbsp. tomato puree

1 tsp. paprika

2 cups dry white wine

6 cups hot beef broth

1 tsp. curry powder

2 bay leaves

salt

6 small, firm, ripe bananas

4 Tbsp. flour

10 Tbsp. cooking oil

2 hardboiled eggs, quartered

1 can green peas

1 red pepper

1 tsp. chopped parsley

PREPARATION

Fry the diced bacon in an ungreased pan for 5 minutes over medium heat. Drain the fat, add the diced ham and sauté for 5 minutes. Set aside.

Melt the butter over medium heat and sauté the chopped onions and green pepper with the crushed garlic for 10 minutest.

Wash the rice well, drain, add to the onions and pepper and cook for 10 minutes, stirring constantly with a wooden spoon.

Add the diced tomato, the tomato puree and the paprika and mix well. Add the wine and allow the alcohol to evaporate for 5 minutes. Add the hot broth, stir and add the curry powder, the bay leaves, and the ham and bacon mixture; add salt to taste. Place in a casserole dish and finish cooking in the oven for approximately 20 minutes at 350°F.

Coat the bananas with flour and fry them in the oil for 5 minutes on each side, until golden.

Serve the rice in individual bowls and distribute the bananas, the quartered eggs and the green peas among the portions. Decorate with thin strips of peeled, fried red pepper and sprinkle with chopped parsley.

> **NOTE**
> It is important to wash the rice to eliminate the starch and prevent it from forming lumps while cooking.

Plymouth,
Still In Use In
Havana.

Cuba has many villas and provincial capitals with old churches and homes. Perhaps the prettiest is Trinidad. It was from here that Hernán Cortés departed to conquer Mexico. The mansions of the rich plantation owners and the ostentation of sugar growers go back to the 18th century when Trinidad was the golden capital of sugar. Dependence on sugar shaped the economic, political, and social history of Cuba, delayed the abolishing of slavery, and fomented colonialism here more than in any other Spanish-American country. In popular tradition and in flattery, sugar and its sweetness are associated with the delights of the mulatto woman. In the cities families had daily recourse to the sweet vendor who advertised his trade with bells and jingles.

Cafiroleta *(Cuba)* #44

INGREDIENTS
(Makes 6 servings)
1¼ lb. sweet potatoes
3 cups water
salt

1 lb. sugar
2 Tbsp. lemon juice
1 cup coconut milk
2 egg yolks, beaten
1 tsp. ground cinnamon

Photo: Panoramic Images

Trinidad, Cuba.

PREPARATION

Peel and cube the sweet potatoes and cook them in two cups of
the water with the salt for 30 minutes over medium heat.
Remove, drain and mash them until smooth. Set aside.

In a thick-bottomed pot, place the sugar, the remaining cup of
water and the lemon juice and boil for 10 minutes over medium
heat, until you get a light syrup.

Cool and add it gradually to the mashed sweet potatoes; add the
coconut milk and mix well.

Cook for 10 minutes over low heat, stirring constantly with a
wooden spoon, until the mixture starts thickening. Gradually
add the beaten egg yolks, stirring to blend them in. Continue
cooking for 10 minutes.

Cool and chill in the fridge for an hour.

Serve in individual bowls, sprinkled with cinnamon.

In a country where the milkman came to the door with his cow and milked
her to order, custards and milk puddings were plentiful. Traditional offerings include *boniatillos* (sweet potato with orange, coconut, or cheese),
frangollo (banana with peanuts), *coquimol* (with coconut milk and cinnamon), puddings, and the typically Spanish-American grated coconut with
cheese. Heat is assuaged with fruit ice creams.

Coffee, rum, and cigars do the rounds after a good Cuban meal. Cuban
coffee is taken in small doses, black and sweet. Throughout the world
Havana is a name synonymous with the very best cigar. The high-quality
smokes are rolled with leaves from the tobacco province of Pinar del Río.

Pineapple Pudding *(Cuba)* #45

INGREDIENTS
(Makes 6 servings)
½ lb. pineapple,
  grated, with juice
4 eggs
1 cup sugar

1 tsp. salt
1 cup milk
8 slices white bread,
  crusts removed
sugar as needed (for
  the mold)

LIQUID CARAMEL
¾ cup sugar
boiling water

Preheat oven to 350°F.

Boil grated pineapple in its own juice for 5 minutes over medium heat. Remove, cool and set aside.

Beat the eggs with the sugar, the salt, the milk and the pineapple. Add the bread, without its crust and crumbled, and stir well to mix all the ingredients. Line the bottom of 6 individual molds with caramel, pour the mixture into them and cook inside another pan filled with water, in a preheated oven, for an hour over at 350°F until the surface of the pudding is golden.

Remove, let it reach room temperature and chill in the fridge for 2 hours.

Pour liquid caramel over it and serve.

LIQUID CARAMEL
Place the sugar in a saucepan and heat for 15 minutes over medium heat, until it takes on a dark brown color without burning. Remove from heat, add some boiling water and mix well. Heat again for 3 minutes, stirring constantly. Remove and allow to cool.

Burnt Coconut (Cuba) #46

NGREDIENTS
(Makes 4 servings)
4 cups milk
¼ can sweetened

coconut cream
12 egg yolks or 7
    whole eggs, well
    beaten

¾ cup flour
1 lb. sugar
½ lb. grated coconut,
    toasted

PREPARATION

Place the milk and half of the coconut cream in a small saucepan and boil until the mixture starts bubbling. In a larger saucepan, mix the egg yolks (or whole eggs if you wish to obtain a thicker cream), the flour and the sugar with the other half of the coconut cream. Slowly add the hot mixture of milk and coconut cream to the egg mixture, stirring constantly for 1 to 2 minutes. Simmer mixture on burner, without stirring, until thick.

Remove from heat. Pour into a bowl and cover with wax paper to prevent it from forming a film over the surface. Once it is cold, sprinkle the toasted grated coconut over cream. Serve cold.

Lobster Varadero (Cuba) #47

INGREDIENTS
(Makes 4 servings)
1 1-lb. lobster tail
1 tsp. ground pepper
salt

4 Tbsp. vegetable oil
1 cup rum
6 Tbsp. Creole Sauce
  (see Recipe #48)
2 cups hot fish broth

1 cup sweet wine

GARNISH
6 white potatoes
2 cups vegetable broth
1 can sweet peas

PREPARATION

Remove the inner fins of the lobster tail. Cut it in thick slices in the spaces between rings and add salt and pepper. Sauté the lobster slices in very hot oil for 5 minutes on each side. Flambé with rum, add the Creole Sauce and the hot fish broth.

Cook, uncovered, for 10 minutes over medium heat; add the wine and allow to reduce for 3 minutes.

Spread the Creole sauce on a serving dish and place the slices of lobster on it.

Serve with a garnish of potatoes, boiled in the broth for 20 minutes over medium heat, and the sweet peas, drained.

> **NOTE**
> Only the lobster tail is used for this dish. Bear in mind that the meat will be done when it separates from the rings.

Creole Sauce (Cuba) #48

INGREDIENTS
(Makes 6 servings)
4 cloves garlic, crushed
8 Tbsp. vegetable oil
2 onions, finely

chopped
2 leeks, finely chopped
2 red peppers, seeded
  & finely chopped
4 tomatoes, peeled,

seeded & diced
3 Tbsp. tomato purée
1 bay leaf
1 Tbsp. salt
1 tsp. ground pepper

3 Tbsp. water

PREPARATION

Fry the crushed cloves of garlic in the oil for 3 minutes over medium heat. Add the chopped onions, leeks and peppers and fry another 10 minutes.

Add the peeled tomatoes, the tomato puree, the bay leaf, the salt and the pepper. Add the water and allow to reduce for 10 minutes. Add more salt if necessary.

> **NOTE**
> Fry the onions and the garlic before the rest of the ingredients to enhance the flavor of the sauce.

Photo: Andina Toby

Hemingway's bar, La Bodeguita Del Medio, Frequented by all visitors to Havana.

One-third of Cuba's population is engaged in the manufacture of cigars and the other two-thirds smoke them, according to a Finnish lady traveler of the 19th century.

Cubans like to eat out of doors to take advantage of the shady verandas and patios. The bars and rum drinks were immortalized by Ernest Hemingway, who wrote three books in Cuba, had as many wives, and knocked back uncountable mojitos and daiquiris. Cuba Libres, popularized during the time of political strife, is mixed using Tropicola (Che Guevara's version of Coca Cola). The national cool drink available on the streets is *guarapo*, iced sugar cane juice pressed for each customer on demand.

El Morro,
Puerto Rico.

*I*n 1898 Cuba and Puerto Rico went from being Spanish colonies to being protectorates of the USA. The battlements and forts of old San Juan are proof of the extremes to which Spain was prepared to go to hold on to its last colony. Eventually Cuba became independent and Puerto Ricans became US citizens. In spite of everything, one hundred years of prosperity have not been enough to wipe out four centuries of Spanish dominion, and Puerto Rico is still Spanish in name, language, traditions, and culture.

Surullitos *(Puerto Rico)* #49

INGREDIENTS
(Makes 10 servings)
2 cups water
salt
2¾ cups corn flour

¼ lb. grated semi-hard cheese
vegetable oil as needed

PREPARATION

Boil the water and salt in a thick-bottomed pot. Add the corn flour in a fine shower, stirring constantly with a wooden spoon to prevent it from forming lumps, and cook for 15 minutes over medium heat, until it thickens.

Remove from heat, add the grated cheese, mix well and allow to cool.

Take small portions of the dough in your hands and form cylinders about 1 to 1¼ inch in diameter and 2½ to 3 inches long. Fry them in very hot oil for 5 minutes, turning them so that they cook evenly, until golden.

Remove and dry the excess oil with paper towels.

Serve hot, as a dish by themselves or as a side dish with other dishes.

> NOTE
> Moisten your hands to make the cylinders to prevent the dough from sticking to them.

The island is surrounded by the brilliant seas shown on tourist brochures. Even though it is the smallest of the Greater Antilles, inland one finds fields with grazing cattle, as if to disprove the belief that all islanders are sea-folk. A central range of mountains — the Two Thousand Hills of Gabriela Mistral's *Puerto Rican Notes* — divides the island in half, the northern part being damp, the southern dry, sharing only plantains and palms. The El Yunque reserve is all that is left of the original forest. From the mangroves of the southwest come oysters, which are prepared raw with coriander and lemon juice.

Tongue Stew *(Puerto Rico)* *#50*

INGREDIENTS
(Makes 4 servings)
1 veal tongue
6 cups water
3 onions
3 carrots, peeled &
   sliced

3 cloves garlic
3 sprigs thyme
1 clove
1 bay leaf, halved
1 Tbsp. vegetable oil
1 Tbsp. brown sugar
salt

GARNISH
1 cup rice
2 cups vegetable broth

Place the tongue, whole, in 6 cups of water with one onion, finely chopped, the sliced carrots, one clove of garlic, crushed, the sprigs of thyme, the clove and the bay leaf halves, and cook, covered, for one hour over medium heat.

Remove the tongue and peel it while hot. Strain and set the broth aside.

Place the oil and the sugar in a thick-bottomed pot and cook for 10 minutes over medium heat until the sugar starts to form caramel. Add the tongue and turn it to coat it with the caramel on both sides. Add the onions and the remaining garlic, finely chopped, and fry them in the cooking juices for 5 minutes over medium heat.

Pour in the reserved cooking broth and heat until the sauce thickens.

Add salt, remove the tongue, cut it in medium slices and cover them with the cooking juices.

Serve with a garnish of rice, boiled in the vegetable broth for 20 minutes over medium heat.

> **NOTE**
> The garnish may be completed with fried macho bananas.

Rice with Gandules (Puerto Rico) #51

INGREDIENTS
(Makes 6 servings)
2 cups water
2 cups coconut milk

2 cups rice
2 onions, finely chopped
2 sprigs thyme, chopped
2 cloves garlic, chopped

1 tsp. salt
2 cans sweet peas

PREPARATION

Place the water and the coconut milk in a pot, cover and heat for 10 minutes over medium heat.

Add the rice, the chopped onions, the chopped thyme and garlic, and the salt. Cook, covered, for 20 minutes over medium heat.

Add the sweet peas and cook, uncovered, for 10 minutes over medium heat, until all the cooking liquid evaporates and the rice is tender.

Serve hot in individual bowls.

Mofongo *(Puerto Rico)* #52

INGREDIENTS
(Makes 3 servings)
3 macho green bananas
2 cups water
salt

vegetable oil as needed
3 cloves garlic
3 tsp. olive oil
3 beef sausages

PREPARATION

Peel the bananas, cut them in 1-inch slices and soak them in water with salt for 20 minutes. Drain, dry and fry them in vegetable oil 3 minutes on each side, over medium heat, without letting them brown. Remove and dry on paper towels. Set aside.

Crush the cloves of garlic in a mortar, gradually adding the olive oil until well mixed. Set aside.

Grind the sausages with the slices of banana and the crushed garlic in food processor until smooth. Remove from the processor, add salt and form 1¼-inch balls. Fry them in vegetable oil for 5 minutes at high. Remove and dry on paper towels. Serve hot.

NOTE
The sausages may be replaced by pork or chicken.
The banana slices are soaked in water with salt so that they will keep their shape during the frying process.

Puerto Rico combines North American comfort and Hispanic tradition. Taverns, rice, seafood stews, tortillas, and fish are reminiscent of Spain. Stews have been given tropical flavor by adding yams, squashes, cassava, and plantains. In wayside inns, much frequented by the islanders, island cooking is the rule. Puerto Rico is the paradise of lobster and piña coladas. Before lunch one can indulge in fish turnovers and *bacalaítos* (cod "fingers") with *surullitos* (fried tidbits). Cuba and Puerto Rico are known for roasted whole suckling pig basted with bitter orange sauce, the ever-present plantains, basted meats, and minced meat pies, invariably seasoned with mortar-

Mint Sticks *(Puerto Rico)* #53

INGREDIENTS
(Makes 10 servings)
5 cups brown sugar
2 Tbsp. glucose

2 Tbsp. mint extract
2 Tbsp. strawberry extract
2 cups water
1 tsp. red food coloring

PREPARATION

In a thick-bottomed pot, mix half of the brown sugar, half of the water, one Tbsp. of glucose and the mint extract. Stir vigorously to mix the glucose with the rest of the ingredients.

Heat over medium heat for 20 minutes, stirring constantly with a wooden spoon, until the caramel starts to thicken.

Remove, cool, pour on a greased surface and spread it with your hands before it cools completely, forming a strip. Set aside.

Follow the same procedure with the remaining ingredients, adding the food coloring and the strawberry extract.

Remove and form another strip with the resulting caramel, as you did before. Set aside.

Before the strips solidify completely, overlap them, forming a bicolor dough.

Stretch the dough again, cut it in strips with a moist knife and knead them forming cylinders about ¾ inch in diameter and 3 inches long. Take 4 or 5 of these and join them by stretching them and twisting their ends together. Allow to solidify.

> NOTE
> Work quickly when making this confection, to prevent the caramel from hardening before you are done.
> Glucose is used to delay drying and make the caramel more elastic.

ground spices available in all friendly eateries. They also share the typical rice and chicken dishes — the rice prepared with a seasoning that adds flavor and color, the chicken fried separately or cooked with vegetables. Less evident but nevertheless present are the ties to Africa in calalu soups, veal with *quimbombo* (a favorite Afro-Caribbean legume), and *mofongo* (mashed plantains with chitterlings and arum), similar to Cuban fufu. Puerto Rican *asopao* (chicken and rice) has its origins in Dominican rice dishes. Desserts confirm Puerto Rico as the great producer of Caribbean vanilla, and provider of happiness in the form of rum and the aroma of good coffee.

Coffee Pie (Puerto Rico) #54

INGREDIENTS
(Makes 8 servings)
CRUST
35 vanilla wafers
1 cup shelled almonds
½ cup shelled walnuts

1 cup shelled peanuts
1 tsp. unsweetened cocoa
1 tsp. grated chocolate
2 Tbsp. light brown
   sugar
2 tsp. vanilla extract

2 tsp. coffee liqueur
2 tsp. rum

FILLING
½ cup butter, at room
   temperature

1 cup sugar
3 tsp. instant coffee
3 tsp. lukewarm water
   eggs

PREPARATION

CRUST

Run vanilla wafers food processor to make crumbs and set aside.

Use food processor to finely chop the almonds, walnuts, and peanuts. Remove from the food processor and place in a bowl. Add the cocoa, the chocolate, the light brown sugar, the vanilla extract, the coffee liqueur, the rum and the vanilla wafer crumbs. Mix well.

Grease a 10-inch pie plate and press the crumb mixture evenly onto the bottom and sides of the pan.

Preheat the oven to 350ºF and bake crust for 15 minutes, until it starts to get golden. Remove and allow to cool.

FILLING

Dissolve coffee in 3 tsp. of lukewarm water and set aside. Beat the butter until creamy. Gradually add the sugar, beat for 10 minutes; add the dissolved coffee and the eggs, one at a time, beating well after each addition.

Pour the mixture into the pie crust and chill for 8 hours.

Remove and serve.

NOTE
The pie may be served with a topping of whipped cream.

Recipe Glossary (Cuba and Puerto Rico)

BIRD PEPPER: a very hot, deep red pepper about the size of a cherry.
CAFIROLETA: a sweet of sweet potatoes, grated coconut, and sugar.
CHILINDRÓN: a dish prepared from chicken, pork, or lamb.
MACHO BANANA: plantain generally longer than the regular ones, which it resembles when green. As the macho banana ripens, its skin, which remains hard, turns yellow, then yellow with brown spots and finally, when ripe, almost black.
MORO, MOROS: rice and beans in various Central American countries.

PAPAYA: fruit of the papaya tree.
GANDULES, GUISANTES: peas.
PIÑA: pineapple.
PLÁTANO: plantain.
SURULLITOS: fried tidbits.
TAMAL EN CAZUELA: tamale cooked in an earthenware pot.

REGION

Machu Picchu, Peru.   Photo: Bill Bachmann

Mamapacha, the Earth, is also revered, especially by the women, at the time of planting, and they talk to her asking her to give them a good harvest, and they make libations of chicha and crushed corn to this end...

—Pablo José de Arriaga, 1564–1622

The Andean region reflects Latin America's diversity and abundance. The Spanish dictionary tells us there are resources and goods worth "a Peru" or "a Potosí." From a gastronomic and geographical perspective Peruvians and Ecuadorians can be divided into coastal people and hill folk, the former more Spanish American, the latter more influenced by the indigenous cultures. In Colombia and Venezuela there are the people of the plains (*llaneros*) between the mountainous backbone and the great tropical forests where roads and tracks come to an abrupt end and inhabitants are sparsely scattered. From Bolivia to Venezuela all the countries own parcels of Amazonia, which has the largest indigenous population, the greatest biodiversity and the most extensive nature reserves.

The Andes region, homogenous and diverse at the same time, is astonishing in its cultural heritage and its variety of landscapes. One surprising aspect are the changing climatic levels one meets as one ascends the Andes mountains. According to the diarist José Oviedo y Baños, "there is nothing sown there which does not draw one's admiration, fertility being aided by the variation in temperance as, in a short distance, and according to the elevation or lowness of the land, one can experience cold, heat or a temperate climate. From this variety of climatic conditions it derives its excellence, for what does not do in one place thrives in another, and what is sterile here is fecund over there." As proof one need only look at the markets, where one can buy potatoes, peppers, corn, beans, and plantains in a variety of colors and flavors, and at the diversity of products from the kitchen that the Andean people sadly miss when they travel abroad.

Corn, potato, and manioc form the trinity of Andean staples. Corn is Meso-American and reached Peru around 2500 BC. The first archaeological evidence of the use of potatoes is, however, from the Peruvian coast (2000 BC). Corn humitas are made from fresh corn, while tamales are of dry cornmeal. Humitas are served on a plate or wrapped in a corn husk. Tamales, known from Catamarca in Argentina to Goiania in Brazil, is a surprise package: the wrapping — corn husk or banana leaves — always encloses a delicious repast. In his *Natural and Moral History of the Indies*,

Photo: Regina María Anzenberger.

Yanomani Indians, Amazon, Venezuela.

the Jesuit Joseph de Acosta mentions that Andean nations have bread, though made not of wheat or rye as in Europe but of corn and manioc.

The pepper is considered king of Latin American spices. Father Bernabé Cobo, who went to Peru as a missionary and naturalist in the 17th century, wrote, "Peppers are such a good spice for the Indians, and make such delicious sauces, that with it they eat everything well."

Through influenced much later by Hispanic and immigrant traditions, the Andean region clings to the culinary memories of pre-Columbian peoples through ancestral foods. The indigenous people's diet consisted of tasty and nutritious foods. It combined grains with legumes and varied the menu with meats, root vegetables, fruits, and herbs. Soups, more or less thick and seasoned, are the Andean specialty. Pre-Hispanic people valued quinoa long before this Andean grain was dismissed by the Conquistadors and much later enthroned by leading nutritionists.

COLOMBIA

A varied geography, a well-stocked natural larder, and generous soil in a land open to the melding of peoples and flavors — all make Colombia one of the culinary hot spots of Latin America. A report on southern America written in 1735 by the Spanish sailor Antonio de Ulloa confirms that cooking is not a trivial affair in Colombian life: with the abundance the country enjoys in all manner of meats, fruit, and fish, one can imagine just how well provided the tables are, which, in the distinguished and comfortable homes, are generously spread with great taste and splendor.

Though Colombia is an equatorial country, its three chains of mountains, two ocean shores, llanos grasslands, and rainforests give it a wide variety of cultural and agricultural aspects. Colombians are experts in adapting ingredients to their tastes and different forms of cooking, creating an extensive and varied collection of recipes that visitors can enjoy as much in the smart restaurants as in humble inns, equally at formal dinners and as between-meal snacks.

The basic components of the Colombian diet are corn, potatoes, manioc, beans, meat, and vegetables, as well as fruit, those mainly used in the kitchen being coconuts, plantains, and avocados. Use of the coconut is a coastal trait and evidence of African influence. Beans are traditional in Antioquia. Different kinds of potato dominate the culinary geography of the central Andes and lend a special character to the boiled meat and vegetables in *ajiaco,* Colombia's national soup and typical of Bogotá. Corn, as Andean and ever-present as potatoes, is dominant in many traditional indigenous recipes that are daily fare, such as *arepas* (a sort of flat, round cornbread) and *mazamorra* (a thick, boiled corn soup). Rice is valued as an accompaniment to main dishes or in regional paellas. Some of the beef, not produced in the Pampas but in mountains, needs seasoning, prior boiling, and roasting to make it more edible. *Fritanga* is the preparation of pork and its derivatives, grilled in various ways, as country food, wayside meals, or on the tables of the wealthy.

Caldas,
Colombia.

Plantains are the great gastronomic experience of Colombia, as they are used in all types of food. Cut up and fried in various ways (toasted, sliced into coin-like rounds, spiced up) they are combined with slices of country cheese and hints of vanilla, cinnamon, or nutmeg.

Colombia is soup country. As simple as it may seem, potato water with a hunk of meaty bone is the most typical food of Colombia. Somewhere between a soup and a boiled stew (*puchero*) is the *sancocho*: meat and vegetables stewed for a long time and seasoned with regional delicacies. It is a variant of the *olla-podrida* so common in medieval Spain, adapted with American seasoning. In the Caribbean they do sancochos with fish and coconut milk; in Cauca Valley with chicken; Andean sancochos have a lot of

Coconut Milk Hen (Colombia) #55

INGREDIENTS
(Makes 6 servings)
1 6½-lb. stewing hen
6 cups coconut milk (see
note)
1 red bell pepper

2 sweet red pepper
2 red onions
2 cloves garlic, crushed
½ tsp. ground black pepper
1 tsp. cumin
salt

GARNISH
2½ cups white rice
5 cups coconut milk
salt and pepper to taste

PREPARATION

Cut the hen in pieces and cook it in 4 cups of the coconut milk for 45 minutes in a covered pot over medium heat.

Remove seeds and membranes from peppers, finely chop them and the onions and add them to the pot together with the crushed garlic, ground black pepper, cumin and salt, and continue cooking for 45 minutes over medium heat, adding the remaining 2 cups of coconut milk.

Remove from heat once the meat of the hen is tender.

GARNISH
Wash the rice with hot water to rid it of the starch and cook it in the boiling coconut milk for 20 minutes. Add salt and pepper.

COCONUT MILK
Break the coconuts (see note under Recipe #19), grate the pulp and put it in a bowl. Add one quart of boiling water for each coconut and let it rest for 10 minutes.

Squeeze between your hands, then strain it through a piece of cloth to separate the pulp from the liquid.

NOTE
When using a chicken instead of a hen, reduce cooking time by half.

Prawn Cebiche *(Colombia) #56*

INGREDIENTS
(Makes 6 servings)
30 fresh prawns
juice of 3 oranges
juice of one lemon

grated rind of one
  orange
grated rind of 3 lemons
1 tsp. sugar
2 onions, finely chopped

2 tomatoes, peeled,
  seeded & cubed
1 Tbsp. hot pepper
2 Tbsp. chopped
  coriander

4 cups water
salt

PREPARATION

Cook the prawns in their shells, in very hot water, for 3 minutes over very high heat. Drain and peel them without removing their ends. Remove the gray vein from their backs and wash them with abundant water.

Place them in a bowl, add the grated rind of the orange and lemon, the juices, the sugar, the chopped onions, the cubed tomatoes, the hot pepper and the chopped coriander. Mix well.

Add salt to taste and allow to marinate for 3 to 4 hours in the fridge.

Serve in individual bowls.

> NOTE
> If you use cooked prawns, skip steps one and two.

---

potato, while on the hot plains plantains and manioc are preferred. The nutritious triple sancocho calls for three kinds of meat, and its best recipe is to be found in the writings of García Márquez: "He also took a demijohn of homemade firewater and the best quality ingredients to make an epic 'sancocho' that could only be created with yard chickens, meat with tender bone, pork fed at the rubbish dump, and vegetables and garden produce from river villages."

In spite of the rich tropical flora, Colombian cooking is not spicy-hot. Peppers, mild or furiously hot, are used according to taste and depending on the cold. Country habits and the climate call for early and substantial breakfasts. These start off with a glass of fresh fruit juice and a bowl of hot soup: meat and potato in the mountains, fish in the coastal region. Seldom does breakfast not include arepas and *huevos perico* (scrambled eggs with onion and tomato). The traditional breakfast in Bogotá includes *almojábanas* (cornmeal tortillas) with cheese. The beverage is coffee, hot

Ajiaco Santafereño *(Colombia) #57*

INGREDIENTS
(Makes 4 servings)
4 chicken breasts
4 cups chicken broth
2 green onions
1 bay leaf

1 small bunch fresh
  sweet basil
2 Tbsp. chopped
  coriander
salt and pepper
4 black-skinned

potatoes
4 white-skinned
  potatoes
4 yellow potatoes
2 ears of corn, sliced
  into quarters

½ cup cream
2 avocados
2 Tbsp. lemon juice
2 Tbsp. capers

Boil the chicken in the broth for 35 minutes over medium heat, together with the onions, basil, coriander and bay leaf to flavor it. Add salt and pepper.

Take the breasts out of the broth and set aside. Strain the broth and discard the vegetables.

Peel the black-skinned potatoes and cook them whole in the broth for 15 minutes. Add the rest of the potatoes, also peeled and whole, and finally the ears of corn, quartered. Continue cooking for 20 minutes. Reserve the broth.

Break the breasts into small pieces using two forks and place in individual casserole dishes, adding a ladleful of hot broth to each. Decorate with a touch of unwhipped cream and the avocados, peeled, quartered and sprinkled with lemon juice.

Serve the potatoes, corn and capers separately.

It can also be served in a casserole dish as in the picture, adding enough broth for 4 servings.

> **NOTE**
> The fresh sweet basil can be replaced by a tsp. ground basil to flavor the broth.

chocolate, or *agua de panela* (brown sugar dissolved in water with a few drops of lemon).

Lunch starts with soup, followed by a main course of potatoes, meat, rice, beans, and vegetables, served in separate helpings. Supper is lighter. If there is no soup there will be more chocolate or meat. Desserts often contain the local preserves, a Spanish tradition but with tropical flavors. Bogotá desserts are farm cheese with honey and junket or *dulce de leche,* a sort of milk and sugar caramel, with figs or whipped cream with sugar, the local equivalent of Spanish custard, typical of Christmas Eve. Rice pudding is a colonial tradition; the Andean form comes with cinnamon and raisins, the coastal version with coconut milk.

Between meals the appetite is deceived (or stimulated, perhaps) with an *empanadilla* (small turnover). The preferred liquor of Colombia is aniseed-flavored rum or regional variants with herbs or fruit, or *canelazo,* the Bogotá pick-me-up. The native alcoholic beverages reported by explorers still raise local spirits: *chicha,* an Andean beer patiently made by fermenting corn, rice, or pineapple, and refreshing local *guarapo,* from sugar cane or pineapple, more or less fermented.

Aborrajados (Colombia) #58

INGREDIENTS
(Makes 6 servings)
6 ripe plantains

1 cup corn oil
2 eggs
4 Tbsp. wheat flour

1 tsp. baking soda
salt
½ lb. soft cheese

PREPARATION

Peel the plantains, slice them lengthwise and fry them in hot oil for 10 minutes until golden.

Beat the eggs with the flour, baking soda and salt. Set aside.

Make the aborrajados by placing a thin slice of soft cheese between two slices of plantain. Sprinkle them with flour, dip them in the egg batter and fry them in hot oil for 5 minutes until golden.

> **TIP**
> In order for this recipe to be successful, the plantains must be ripe and the cheese must be firm.

Chocolate is still a favorite at the Colombian table. In colonial days the frothy cup of hot chocolate was taken at the end of the Bogotá siesta. In the villages it was taken at the end of saying the Rosary and was sold on the streets at all times. Coffee is cultivated in Andean valleys and the *tinto,* the demitasse, is drunk any time and is always offered to visitors.

To sate the appetite or put cravings to rest there are the ever-present itinerant roadside carts offering empanadas, fried buns, *bolos* (corn-, plantain-, or aniseed-flavoured cheese fritters wrapped in corn husks), and the typically coastal *carimañolas* (a Moorish kebab with fried manioc), good for accompanying fritangas. Tamales and arepas are standbys that rise above the street-vending scene to accompany Christmas and New Year meals.

Arepas are a a cornbread relative of the Mexican tortilla but too thick to roll up around fillings. Depending on the region they maybe sweet or salty and vary in recipe and size. Those on the coast are stuffed with egg.

Rice pudding *(Colombia)* #59

INGREDIENTS
(Makes 6 servings)
1 cup rice
2 cups milk

1 cup water
¾ cup sugar
⅓ cup seedless white
    raisins

salt
2 cinnamon sticks
2 tsp. ground cinnamon

PREPARATION

Wash the rice and drain it. Place it in a thick-bottomed pot with one cup of milk and one of water and cook for 20 minutes over medium heat, until the rice absorbs the liquid.

Bring the heat down, add another cup of milk, the sugar, the raisins, a pinch of salt and the cinnamon sticks. Stir constantly with a wooden spoon for 15 minutes until the rice is cooked and juicy.

Remove the cinnamon sticks and allow to cool.

Serve in individual dessert dishes, sprinkled with ground cinnamon.

NOTE
It is important to add the sugar at the final stage to prevent the rice from hardening.

Regional variations in tamales lie in the filling (nearly always of rice) and the wrapping (usually banana leaves). The ways of tying them up vary according to the contents, like the various methods for sealing Argentine empanadas. Tamales from the Bogotá plateau are made from ground sweet corn, wrapped in corn husks, and closed without ties. The small tamale from the Caribbean (*bollolimpio*) is made of corn, neither sweet nor salty, and accompanies fried food, roast meat, and fish stews (*sancochos*).

Cartagena was one of the continent's entry points. Here bishops and missionary friars, viceroys and the Inquisition, merchants and fortune-hunting adventurers all came ashore. The narrow streets and churches, the fairs and inns all came to life whenever the galleons arrived. This port, the most fortified in all Spanish America, concluded the crossing to the Indies; in other words, the measly onboard rations came to an end and the voyager could now feast on juicy fruit and succulent dishes. Starting from Cartagena the Spaniards conquered Great Colombia and delighted in the rich

Snail Meat Balls (Colombia) #60

INGREDIENTS
(Makes 4 servings)
1 lb. snails
2 cups vegetable broth
2 black-skinned
  potatoes

1 slice of bread
1 onion
1 hot green pepper
1 hot pepper
1 green pepper
2 cloves garlic

1 Tbsp. chopped
  coriander
salt and pepper
1 egg
1½ cups olive oil

FOR CLEANING SNAILS
rock salt as needed
vinegar as needed

GARNISH
Boiled lentils

Clean the snails and cook in the broth over moderate heat for one hour. Remove from heat, let them cool to warm temperature, grind them in a food processor for 1 minute, place them in a bowl and set aside.

Peel the potatoes, boil them and cube them. Cube the slice of bread.

Finely chop the onion, the peppers — without seeds or membranes — and the garlic. Add all ingredients to the snail paste, add the coriander, salt and pepper. Beat the egg and blend it in.

Knead the preparation thoroughly and form into balls, about 1½ inches in diameter. Fry them in hot oil for 15 minutes until golden.

Serve over a bed of boiled lentils.

CLEANING THE SNAILS

Place the snails in a loosely covered container for 8 days; select those which are closed by a thick mucous film, removing it. Wash them several times with warm water, and discard those that have not shown their heads.

Place them in water with rock salt and vinegar and let them soak for an hour, until they have oozed all their matter; wash them again to remove any leftover mucus.

Put the snails in a pan, cover with water and boil for 5 minutes over medium heat until they come out of their shells; take to maximum heat so they cook before they have a chance to get into their shells again, and allow to boil for 20 minutes. Remove from heat and discard shells.

---

peninsular stews with corn, manioc, and fruit. This was also the port of entry for food items not available in the Americas — garlic, onions, chick peas. Spanish cookery did not arrive with fixed recipes. In the beginning, since there was not enough of the traditional foods to go around, one had to be content with what the land provided. Eventually the local fare would be able to satisfy even the most demanding tastes of recent arrivals.

From the Caribbean shores slaves were marched inland to work on plantations, consolidating the mix of peoples, customs, and foods. Those who escaped from the plantations founded *palenques* (communities) where traditions were maintained and the land prepared for the sowing of crops that would establish the regional dishes. Even today, the descendants of these escaped slaves prepare delicious fruit confections, coconut sweets, and penny rolls, and can be seen on the beaches gracefully balancing baskets on their heads, selling local fruit to the sunbathers.

In the Caribbean region rice and coconut are used in delicious ways. The sea provides fish and shellfish, which are fried, baked, or stewed in casseroles with coconut milk. Those from Barranquilla prefer mullet and rice, while the people of Cartagena go for shad sancocho. A vast area along the Atlantic coast, sometimes called Colombia's Caribbean, spreads from the foot of the Andes to the floodplain of the Magdalena River. In the 19th century when populous Barranquilla became the capital of maritime Colombia, those traveling to Bogotá journeyed up this Colombian Danube in uncomfortable scows where they were offered jerked beef soup, lentils, and beans. They passed Santa Cruz de Mompox, an ancient colonial settlement where Holy Week is still celebrated with the traditional neighborly exchange of sweets and fruit in commemoration of the Last Supper.

Few mountain ranges in the world are as productive as those of Colombia. With a climate varying according to elevation, the slopes offer perfect conditions for growing valuable crops like cocoa, coffee, corn, and potatoes, as well as many fruits and vegetables. The travel guides tell of cold to temperate weather; damp, high montane plateaus; fertile valleys with wooded slopes; high peaks (*páramos*); and permanently snow-capped volcanoes, all within a country about the size of Italy. The Andean hub is Cundinamarca and the fertile savannah of Bogotá. Around the capital there are other culinary and tourist regions: the Santanderes to the north; west, inland Antioquia (home of Medellín), Viejo Caldas, the central coffee region, and Alto Cauca; southwards Alto Magdalena, also known as Gran Tolima.

The writer and essayist Germán Arciniegas reminds us that Colombia does not begin at the Atlantic or Pacific ocean shores but at the top of the Andes where Bogotá is situated. In 1537, in search of gold and emeralds, a detachment of Spaniards penetrated the cordillera, suffering the effects of hunger. They founded Santafe de Bogotá at 8,500 feet elevation, in the territory of peaceful Indians who planted corn once a year, cooked potatoes and mazamorras, salted meat, made manioc bread, and drank chicha. Bogotá today is a modern city with colonial airs, especially in the Candelaria suburb. It offers all the cultural and culinary attractions of a great capital city. It is also home to a famous market where one can eat anything one pleases in a casual atmosphere. Farther up at 9,000 feet sits Tunja, the

Cartagena de
Indias, Colombia.

capital of Bocayá, known for its churches and convents. Between the soups
and baked cheesecakes of Bogotá and Bocayá's pork and barley soups
with corn lie 150 miles of extraordinary mountain scenery.

The twin provinces of the Santanderes rising in steps from Bogotá north-
wards have delicious cooking, including goat prepared many ways, even a
stew colored by the animal's own blood. But the most curious regional
food is edible ants. Somebody found that the tastiest part of their anato-
my was the abdomen and called them *culonas* (big-bottomed). From indigenous barbecues where they were roasted to a crisp right at the anthill, to
the shelves of urban supermarkets where they are sold packed and ready
to nibble on, these ants have followed a long gastronomic trail.

Egg Arepa (Colombia) #61

INGREDIENTS
(Makes 4 servings)
1 cup corn flour (not cornmeal)
1 cup water

salt and pepper
1¼ cups olive oil
4 eggs
1 head lettuce

Mix the corn flour with the salt, pepper and water at room temperature until the dough is smooth and firm. Let rest for 10 minutes, divide it in four parts and form it into balls.

Shape the arepas by flattening them with moistened hands until they form a disc approximately 2½ inches in diameter and ³⁄₁₆ inches thick.

Fry them in hot oil so that they cook evenly; once they come up to the surface, remove them and drain them on paper towels.

Make a small incision on the edge of each arepa to fill them, stand them on edge and break an egg into each of them, adding a tsp. salt water to prevent the white from mixing with the yolk.

Close the opening with a little fresh dough and fry them for a couple of minutes, until golden. Serve on a bed of lettuce leaves. They can also be served with fried plantain.

In the mid-19th century settlers from Antioquia ascended the Cauca River to plant corn and beans. They conquered Viejo Caldas with pork suet, bacon, and helpings of beans. By some strange gastronomic coincidence, where there are beans there are also sausages, and Antioquia celebrates this fact in kitchens and restaurants. Beans, like the *feijao* of Brazil, are an everyday food, though here they like the sweetish flavor imparted by plantains.

In 1801, before Viejo Caldas became a coffee paradise, Baron von Humboldt crossed the craggy Quindio cordillera and, by his own account, congratulated himself for discovering one of the world's richest sources of useful and curious plants. Today agro-tourism seeks to share this regional treasure by offering a trail through cane thickets, plantations, and villages of singular beauty such as Salento and Montenegro. The typical dish of the coffee region of Antioquia is the *bandeja paisa*. It can be found in Medellín's restaurants but evolved to grace the tables of country homes with the produce of the land: beans and rice, pork, plantains, and fried eggs.

About 1867 the writer Jorge Isaacs told of the natural and social setting of the Cauca Valley in *María,* one of Colombia's best known books. In a room whose furnishings had been reduced to old sofas, pictures of Quito's saints, and tables adorned with bowls of plaster fruit and parrots, he is served an unpretentious but well-prepared meal: "The tortilla soup

Bollolimpio *(Colombia)* *#62*

INGREDIENTS
(Makes 4 servings)
8 cups kernels of yellow corn
6 cups water

2 cups vegetable broth
2 cloves garlic
salt and pepper
16 corn husks

PREPARATION

Soak the kernels of corn in water for 8 hours; remove any dirt, drain and cook in the vegetable broth over medium heat for 30 minutes.

Cool, drain the kernels and reserve the broth.

Process the kernels together with the garlic. Add salt and pepper and knead until smooth.

Wash the husks and dry them with paper towels. Mound two Tbsp. of the mixture in the center of each husk, cover with another, folding them downwards to envelope the mixture, and tie them with cotton twine.

Cook in the boiling broth for 25 to 30 minutes. Remove from the broth and serve without the twine.

---

seasoned with fresh herbs from the garden; the fried plantains with shredded meat and cornmeal buns; the excellent local chocolate; the hard cheese, the milk bread, and the water served in a huge, ancient silver tankard left nothing to be desired." Black cooks roasted cheeses, fried buns and *pandebonos* (manioc bread), and boiled jellies.

The Cauca Valley region is the heart of Colombian sugar production. The regional capital is Cali, which took over from beautiful colonial Popayán, founded in 1537 astride the King's Highway between Cartagena and Quito. If in these two capitals of Cauca *pipián* tamales (stuffed with spicy stew) reign, in Alto Magdalena the Tolima tamale is preferred. A majestic cordillera separates these tasty holdovers from Andean cultures. Together with the Tolima tamale, stuffed suckling pig is much appreciated. No New

Cartagena.

Meringues with Mulberry Sauce

(Colombia) #63

INGREDIENTS
(Makes 6 servings)
MERINGUE
6 egg whites
⅛ tsp. cream of tartar
1⅛ cup sugar

½ tsp. vanilla extract
½ tsp. anise extract
1 tsp. lemon juice
½ Tbsp. butter (for the
  mold)

MULBERRY SAUCE
½ lb. mulberries
1⅛ cup sugar
¼ cup water

Beat the egg whites with the cream of tartar until stiff; gradually add sugar, lemon juice, vanilla and anise extracts, and continue beating until firm.

Place the meringue in a cake decorating bag with a fluted tip and form small scallops on a greased cookie sheet. Bake in pre-heated oven at 350°F for 10 minutes.

Turn off the oven and leave the meringues in for 40 minutes, until dry, firm and crunchy.

Serve freshly made with cold mulberry sauce.

TIP
In order for the whites to become firm they must be at room temperature.

MULBERRY SAUCE
Wash and clean the mulberries. Place them in a pan with the water and sugar and boil for 10 minutes, skimming the foam from the surface with a wooden spoon.

Year's feast is complete without these delights, which are nationally famous. The piglet is roasted and presented whole at the table, as delectable as the best suckling pigs of Segovia.

When one descends from the valley of Bogotá towards Villavicencio, capital of the Meta, half the country has yet to be visited: Colombia's far east is seldom toured because of the lack of communications and services. This cattle-raising region (the Llanos) and forested Amazonia, cut up into cattle stations and natural reserves, ends on the banks of the Orinoco — the "stabbing dagger of water," according to the poet Eduardo Carranza — at distant Leticia, the Punta Arenas of Colombia, where the traveler can sample fish from the Amazon. On the farms in the Llanos veal is roasted skewered on sticks stuck into the ground around the fire at long drawn-out feasts that enliven family or social get-togethers.

In the mid-19th century travelers on the Llanos were known to veer from their course in order to visit a well-provided village where they could get *casabe,* a bread made out of wild manioc (*mandioca brava*), the poison of which was neutralized by indigenous know-how. Casabe goes with fish, turtle eggs, and any other food. It replaces arepas and is as essential as manioc flour in the Brazilian jungles.

PERU

*P*eru was the Conquest's first great South American storehouse. The Incas who ruled in the central Andes may not have known about the wheel but they were specialists in preserving foods: salted meats, pre-cooked herbs, dried potatoes. "Flouring" fish with corn and cassava facilitated its transport to market and to the state granaries where surpluses were stored against times of poor harvests. Five centuries later Peru is still the world's leading producer of fish meal, and jerked meat is still the traditional meat for the South American stew-pot. *Chuño* is potato dehydrated by the combined effects of freeze-drying at night and sun-drying by day, and its use in the kitchen has not varied greatly.

Peruvian cooking is either maritime, hill-type, or tropical. Though tour guides point out natives wrapped in colorful blankets and ponchos, Peru is an equatorial country. Rural people make their dishes with whatever the land has produced, from time immemorial. Urban dwellers have well-stocked markets at hand where industrially produced foods from other provinces are readily available. They reserve their more elaborate dishes for special occasions.

The Pacific is an ocean of cold waters and desert shores. Fish has always been an important source of food for Peruvians and for millions of seabirds that deposited guano. Peru's coastal civilizations — Moche, famous for ceramics, in the north; Nazca, known for the undecipherable "lines" that can be seen from the air, in the south — were already using guano intensively as fertilizer in ancient times.

As one moves into the hills, fish becomes less important, giving pride of place to potatoes and corn, crops that do well at higher elevations. The hill people, as Andean folk are known, also appreciate dried meat and the flesh of the guinea pig or *cavy,* which bygone generations sacrificed to the gods but today is eaten with potatoes, roasted à la Cuzco, stewed, or even fried with hot peppers. On the eastern forested Amazon slopes plantains are king, fried, stewed or baked with cinnamon. Roasted or mashed with chitterlings and butter they are called *tacachos,* good with morning coffee. The classic dish on the coast is *cebiche* (ceviche), made with very fresh

Photo: Gerard Sioen-Ag. Anzenberger

Lake Titicaca,
Peru.

corvina, a Pacific fish, macerated in lemon juice. This eating habit of the Peruvians is shared by other fish-eating people of the Pacific and suggests a rudimentary form of preparing food without the use of heat. Indigenous cebiches are eaten on the beach where the freshly caught fish is immediately washed, cut up, and sprinkled with lemon juice. For the more sophisticated it can be covered with sliced onion, peppers, and coriander, and left to macerate in lemon juice for a few hours. Though fish is fresher on the coast, *cebicherías* have turned it into the national dish. Fish and seafood are also prepared in hot soups such as *parihuela,* the Peruvian bouillabaisse. Prawns, flavored in *chupes* (stews) and *ocopas* (sauces made of peppers, peanuts, garlic, and onions), enlivened the menus of coastal pre-Incan cultures.

Throughout history, Amazonia has been more isolated than the coast and this produced different eating habits. Its Peruvian capital is Iquitos, the fevered Omagua of colonial goldseekers' fiction. It was here that the crazed

Peruvian Cebiche (Peru) #64

INGREDIENTS
(Makes 4 servings)
2 lb. sole or blenny,
  boned
2 medium onions

2 yellow peppers
1 red or green hot
  pepper
juice of 6 lemons
2 cloves garlic

1 tsp. ground pepper
lettuce leaves as needed
2 Tbsp. chopped
  parsley
salt and pepper

GARNISH
2 white potatoes
2 ears of corn
2 sweet potatoes

PREPARATION

Remove the seeds and membranes from the peppers; cube the yellow peppers and finely chop the hot pepper. Set aside.

Cut the fish in small pieces, add salt and pepper, the crushed cloves of garlic, and the ground pepper, and cover with the hot pepper. Pour the lemon juice over it, adding the yellow peppers and the onions, finely sliced. Allow to marinate in the fridge for 2 hours.

Cook the potatoes and the sweet potatoes separately, boiling them, whole and in their jackets, in water with salt for 20 minutes over medium heat. Cool, peel and cut them in thin slices.

Cut the ears of corn in small pieces and boil them in water with a tsp. of salt for 10 minutes over medium heat.

Serve on a bed of lettuce leaves, sprinkling the cebiche with finely chopped parsley.

> **Tip**
> The fish should not be marinated over 2 hours for the cebiche to be ready.

Lope de Aguirre started to plan the death of the governor, Pedro de Ursúa, leader of the unfortunate expedition sent to take possession of those lands. The natives provided them with food that has changed little since then: fish, fruit, and manioc flour. They also obtained butter and turtle eggs, "and with their meat and a lot of corn which there was there, usually fed on fritters and pies and many types of stews and pottages." Tired of the governor keeping the best bits for himself, the plotters killed him on the night of the Feast of the Circumcision of 1561, "and he rose and tried to flee but fell dead amongst the pots in which his food was being prepared."

The Cuzco region, reached along the course of the upper Urubamba River, condenses all the tourist attractions of Peru: archaeology (the Inca ruins of Machu Picchu, only discovered in 1911), historic trails (the Inca trail), mountain railways, colonial architecture, colorful local markets and eateries offering stewed lamb, roast meats, and, if there is still room for more, *aguaymanto,* the Andean cherry. The *pachamanca* (Quechua for earthenware pot) is cooked underground surrounded by volcanic rocks which, once glowing, keep the food hot and maintain its nutritive value. This mountain *curanto* has both a ritual and symbolic character. In the countryside it was prepared for celebrations of religious and festive occasions, cooking in the very heart of the earth those foods which Pachamama

Chorrillana *(Peru)* #65

INGREDIENTS
(Makes 6 servings)
6 tomatoes
6 onions
1 yellow pepper

1 red pepper
4 Tbsp. olive oil
2 cloves garlic
6 flounder fillets
1 Tbsp. oregano

1 cup white wine
1 cup fish broth (see
   Recipe #67)
4 boiled white potatoes
salt and pepper

PREPARATION

Peel three tomatoes, seed them and cube them. Finely chop the onions and set aside.

Roast the peppers in hot oven (450ºF) for 25 minutes, peel them, seed them, remove the membranes and cut them in strips.

Place the oil in a thick-bottomed pan, sauté the cloves of garlic until golden and spread the cubed tomatoes, chopped onions and fillets in layers. Add the remaining tomatoes in halves, peeled and seeded, the pepper strips, oregano, white wine and fish broth. Add salt and pepper and simmer for 25 minutes.

Serve garnished with boiled white potatoes.

---

dispenses to man. The pachamanca is more traditional in Ayacucho (the Guamanga of old) and Guancavelica, memorable towns on the Inca Trail.

Touristically speaking, Huancayo is not notable as Cuzco, but this mountain capital gives its name to potatoes *á la huancaína,* found in every roadside eatery from Tumbes to Tacna and beyond. To capture the scent of American cinnamon Pizarro's Spaniards had to reach Cajamarca. Three centuries later Humboldt would come here to view the gardens of Atahualpa's old home where, according to the Peruvian Poma de Ayala, the Incas awaited Pizarro with produce from his garden and roast ducks.

Arequipa, of the Misti volcano and the convent-village of Santa Catalina, enjoys foods from both the sea and the hills. It is a land of marinades and

Huancaína Potatoes (Peru) #66

INGREDIENTS
(Makes 6 servings)
6 tomasa white potatoes
6 yellow potatoes
6 huayro potatoes

HUANCAÍNA SAUCE
6 yellow peppers
4 eggs
10.5 oz. cream cheese
1¼ cups evaporated milk
6 Tbsp. olive oil

4 soda crackers
1 tsp. sugar
juice of one lemon
3.5 oz. pitted green
   olives
6 leaves curly lettuce

2 Tbsp. chopped parsley
salt and pepper

PREPARATION

Place the different types of potatoes, whole and unpeeled, in different pots. Barely cover them with water, add salt and boil for about 20 minutes over low heat. Cool, peel and slice. Set aside.

HUANCAÍNA SAUCE

Cut the peppers in half, seed them and remove the membranes.

Place them in a pot, barely cover them with water, add sugar and boil for 15 minutes over medium heat until tender. Cool and peel.

Boil the eggs during 10 minutes over medium heat; separate the yolks.

Put the peppers, cream cheese, yolks, quartered crackers, evaporated milk and oil through the blender. Add salt and pepper and continue blending until you get a creamy sauce. Add the juice of one lemon and set aside.

Distribute the potatoes on a bed of lettuce leaves, alternating the white, yellow and huayro potatoes. Cover with the huancaína sauce and decorate with olives and chopped parsley.

NOTE
The potatoes must be cooked separately so that each variety may retain its flavor. Evaporated milk may be replaced by regular cow's milk.

Shrimp Chupe (Peru) #67

INGREDIENTS
(Makes 4 servings)
1¼ lb. shrimp
¾ cup rice
1 onion
4 yellow potatoes
4 cups fish broth

½ cup green peas
2 cloves garlic
1 egg
1 Tbsp. tomato purée
2 Tbsp. evaporated milk
¼ lb. soft cheese
¼ lb. Parmesan cheese

4 Tbsp. butter
2 Tbsp. chopped
   coriander
1 tsp. ground pepper
flour as needed
salt and pepper

FISH BROTH
1 fish head and tail
6 cups water
1 carrot
1 celery stalk
1 onion
1 Tbsp. salt

PREPARATION

Finely chop the onion and sauté it in one Tbsp. of butter for 10 minutes over medium heat, together with the crushed garlic. Add the tomato sauce, the ground pepper and the salt. Add the rice, green peas, potatoes, peeled and diced, and the fish broth. Simmer for 20 minutes. Add the egg, slightly beaten, stir and add the evaporated milk, a Tbsp. coriander and the soft cheese, cubed. Finish cooking for 1 minute, stirring constantly with a wooden spoon.

Clean the shrimp, coat them with flour, fry them in the remaining butter for 5 minutes over high heat and add them to the mixture.

Serve in individual bowls, sprinkling with grated Parmesan cheese and the remaining coriander.

FISH BROTH
Boil the fish head and tail in water with salt, together with the carrot, celery and onion, for 40 minutes over medium heat.

> **TIP**
> As you add the egg, slightly beaten, stir constantly so that it will set in strings.

---

stews, of stuffed ocoto peppers, of ocopas, chupes, and prawn picantes. For dessert, the mountain route offers Arequipa's marzipans, Ayacucho's candied fruit, Cuzco's *guisado* (a peach confection), Huaynuco's sugar candies, and the *guaguas* from Todos los Santos for festive occasions.

Although the Inca capital was in the mountains, Pizarro and his conquistadors founded their own near the coast and even today it is the only Andean capital with sea air. In Lima one can enjoy the national cooking as well as specialties of other regions, from international and nouvelle cuisine to simple restaurants where the country's fare is prepared — ceviches, *huariques,* and *picanterías. Chifas* are Chinese restaurants that started as poor people's restaurants. Japanese cuisine sticks to the classic fare but also adds variation on the flavors of local cooking called *nikkei.* Based on local produce from the sea, oriental cooking is well established in Peru. Unlike other South American countries it arrived early on and is not considered exotic nor an immigrant cuisine but a post-colonial mix.

Lima is recognized by its historic walls decorated by the Spaniards with lattice-work and baroque trimmings, by the closed-in balconies reminiscent of mameluke Egypt's lookouts, and by the reputation of its convents.

Natillas Piuranas (Peru) #68

INGREDIENTS
(Makes 4 servings)
2 cups brown sugar

2 cups milk
2 cups evaporated milk
½ tsp. yeast

1 cup chopped walnuts
water as needed

PREPARATION

Place the sugar in a thick-bottomed pot, add half a cup of water and boil for 30 minutes over medium heat, stirring constantly with a wooden spoon to prevent the sugar from burning.

In another saucepan, mix the milk with the evaporated milk and the yeast, previously dissolved in a demitasse of lukewarm water, and keep over medium heat for 10 minutes, until it is about to boil.

Pour the milk over the sugar and continue simmering for 10 minutes, stirring constantly until it thickens and takes on a golden color.

Finally, add the chopped walnuts and let it cook for approximately 45 minutes over medium heat. Cool in the fridge and serve in individual dessert dishes.

NOTE
The best custard (*natillas*) is made with goat's milk.

According to Vázquez de Espinosa, who recorded American life at the beginning of the 17th century, Lima's convents exceed those of Spain in ornament and ostentation "and especially the nuns, as each regales one with the compliment of gifts of aromas, rich and sweet waters, and are beyond endearing."

Lima was the closest thing to a courtly capital the Americas had. There one fed better than in any other city and it is still considered the Latin American capital of desserts and confections. The national sweet, prepared in aristocratic and convent kitchens, is a happy convergence of Arabic, Spanish, and indigenous contributions. While not deprecating cassava and camote — root vegetables that early Peruvians already used in the making of sweets — it consecrated sugar cane syrup, brown sugar, cinnamon, aniseed, almonds, milk, and fruit. The battery of sweets and desserts is based on cornmeal porridge, rice puddings (the Andean dessert par excellence), ladyfingers, custards, jam-filled

Carapulcra *(Peru) #69*

INGREDIENTS
(Makes 4 servings)
14 oz. pork loin
½ chicken

1 onion
1 Tbsp. panca pepper
2 cloves garlic
14 oz. dried potatoes

(*papa seca*)
1 cup roasted peanuts
1 tsp. cumin
1 clove

1 cinnamon stick
1 cup sweet wine
6 Tbsp. olive oil
salt and pepper

PREPARATION

Cut the chicken and the pork loin in small pieces and fry them in half the oil for 5 minutes, over high heat, until golden. Set aside.

Place the remaining oil in a thick-bottomed pot and fry the finely chopped onion and the crushed garlic for 15 minutes over medium heat. Add the panca pepper, cumin, cinnamon and clove. Add salt and pepper, add the pieces of meat and continue cooking for 5 minutes over medium heat.

Add the dried potatoes, previously hydrated; cover with water and simmer, covered, for 45 minutes until the meats are tender.

Process the peanuts and add them, together with the wine, about 10 minutes before cooking is complete.

Remove the cinnamon stick and clove before serving.

> **NOTE**
> The dried potatoes or *papa seca* must be hydrated in lukewarm water for an hour. Drain and use. They may be replaced by fresh sliced potatoes in slices; in this case add them 15 mins. before the end of cooking time.

cookies, nougats, caramels, sugar cane chews, coconut candy, jam tarts, cakes, creams, and fruit jams (Peruvian achras, chirimoyas, custard-apples). Cheese and *picarones* (fried dough) are accompanied by cane syrup.

Peruvian kitchens are active from early in the day. To prepare the soups, hot stones are placed in earthenware pots. This is how *kalapurca* (sometimes *carapulcra*) started. It is prepared with dehydrated potato, pork, and peppers (pre-Inca versions had guinea pigs in lieu of the Spaniards' pork). The stews prepared by the natives were *locro* (llama jerky, potatoes, and peppers) and chupes of meat or fish. Boiled meats and vegetables are typically Spanish-American and a derivation of Hispanic *pucheros,* but Peruvianized with cassava, potatoes, sweet potatoes, and local herbs. Marinading fish, chicken, or game is borrowed from Spanish cookery. Also popular are *anticuchos* (pieces of ox heart on a spit, spiced with panca

Suspiros de Limeñas *(Peru)* #70

INGREDIENTS
(Makes 6 servings)
6 eggs
1 cup condensed milk

1 cup whipping cream
1 tsp. vanilla extract
1 Tbsp. ground
cinnamon

SYRUP
1 cup sugar
¼ cup sweet wine

PREPARATION

Separate the yolks from the whites. Place the yolks in a stainless steel bowl on the stove, together with the condensed milk, the cream and the vanilla extract and beat for 20 minutes over medium heat.

In a small saucepan, cover the sugar with the wine and boil approximately 15 minutes, without stirring it to prevent it from crystallizing, until it becomes a syrup thick enough to form small balls.

Beat the egg whites until they are firm and form peaks, and gradually pour the syrup into them without stopping beating until the meringue cools.

Distribute it over the individual servings, sprinkle with cinnamon and serve. It can be served with fresh fruit.

TIP
To test the cooking point of the syrup, place a tsp. of it in cold water; as you take it between your fingers you should be able to form it into a soft ball.

Tacu Tacu *(Peru)* #71

INGREDIENTS
(Makes 4 servings)
1 cup white rice
1 cup beans

1 onion
2 yellow peppers
4 sirloin steaks
4 green bananas

4 eggs
½ cup olive oil
water as needed
salt and pepper

PREPARATION

Cook the rice in 4 cups of water and a Tbsp. of salt for 20 minutes over medium heat; strain and set aside.

Cook the beans in 4 cups of water for one hour over medium heat. Remove from heat and drain. Mix the rice and the beans and fry them in half of the oil, very hot, for 10 minutes. Set aside.

Cut the peppers, remove their seeds and membranes and chop them finely. Chop the onion finely, add it and the peppers to the mixture and stir.

Cook the steaks on a grill for 10 minutes at high; add salt and pepper.

Serve the steaks with the rice and beans, accompanied with a garnish of eggs and green bananas, fried in the remaining oil for 5 minutes at high.

---

peppers and cooked over hot coals), *causa* (a sort of mashed potato stuffed with meat or fish), and *olluquito* (stews of potatoes and dried meat).

Nearly all pre-Hispanic meats adopted garlic and onions, "because onions, garlic and carrots grow no better in Spain than they do in Piru [*sic*]," according to Father Acosta. Rice is present in *caucau* (minced tripe), chicken *ají* (joints of chicken with hot pepper sauce), and *secos,* a term in Peru and Bolivia that refers simply to the main course but can also mean meat stewed with rice. Rice with chicken is the celebratory food for the Feast of San Juan (hence *juanes* in Amazonia). Northern rice is cooked with prawns in Piura, with duck in Chiclayo, with young goat in Trujillo. Trujillo was founded on ancient Chan Chan, the capital of pre-Inca Chimu, one of the most important archaeological sites in South America.

Rabbit Stew (Peru) #72

INGREDIENTS
(Makes 4 servings)
1 3-lb. rabbit
8 small onions
1 ½-lb. slice of ham

4 cloves garlic
4 Tbsp. olive oil
2 Tbsp. vinegar
2 cups dry white wine
1 tsp. ground cumin

1 tsp. oregano
1 tsp. rosemary
2 Tbsp. finely chopped
  parsley
1 cup pitted black

olives
salt and pepper

6 tomasa white
  potatoes, boiled

Photo: Gerard Sioen/Ag. Anzenberger

Taquili Island,
Lake Titicaca,
Peru.

Preparation

Cut the rabbit in 8 pieces, add salt and pepper, the crushed garlic, cumin, oregano and rosemary. Add three Tbsp. oil and the vinegar. Marinate for 12 hours in a covered container in the fridge. Turn the pieces every four hours so that they will take on the flavors and aromas of the seasonings evenly. Take the pieces out of the marinade, dry them with paper towels and set the marinade aside.

Cube the ham and fry it in the remaining oil for 5 minutes at high; add the pieces of rabbit, fry them for 5 minutes on each side at high until golden; remove them.

Place the pieces of rabbit in a thick-bottomed pot, add the ham, the wine, the whole onions and the marinade. Simmer for 2 hours, until the rabbit is tender. Remove the pieces of rabbit and continue cooking until the sauce thickens.

Serve with a garnish of boiled potatoes, decorated with the pitted olives, and sprinkled with chopped parsley.

The joy of popular feasts is associated with consumption of native *chichas* and Spanish American fire-waters. Pisco is distilled from the Iquique grapes as the port of Magdalena de Pisco has been called since the late 16th century, "where many ships come to load the wine from its valleys." Later the name was applied to other spirits from Peru and Chile. *Chicha* is the native beer that to the diarist Gonzalo Fernández de Oviedo is superior to that of Flanders. Chichas can be refreshing or inebriating according to the fruit or the degree of fermentation reached. It is brewed from sugar cane juice (*guarapo*), fermented cassava (*masato*), or from the fruit of palms. The favorite is *chicha morada* from dark red corn and *chicha de jora* from yellow corn, a domestically drunk aperitif.

Photo: Gerard Sioen-Ag. Anzenberger

Aruba, a Dutch island off Venezuela.

*T*hree or four Venezuelas began to meld during the time of Bolivar: the Andean with that of the Llanos, the eastern with the Guianan, and that of Coria with Zulia. Tourism pamphlets promote the accessible Venezuela of the Caribbean, rather than the out-of-the-way Orinoco delta.

At mealtimes just about everyone lines up for their *arepas: arepitas con perico* (scrambled eggs — a must at breakfast), or stuffed and laced with hot sauces, or with fried plantains (the popular *tostones*). Arepas, always warm, replace wheat bread and vindicate humble cornmeal.

Pabellón *(Venezuela)* #73

INGREDIENTS
(Makes 8 servings)
2¼ lb. flank steak
4 cups beef broth
2 tomatoes, peeled, seeded & cubed
2 onions, finely chopped
2 cloves garlic, finely chopped
salt and pepper
1 cup olive oil
1 cup white rice
2 cups water
2 plantains or bananas
8 fried eggs
Caraotas (Recipe #74)

PREPARATION

Cut the beef in chunks, place it in a pot with the broth, cover and boil for about 1½ hours over medium heat, until tender. Remove from heat, allow to cool, and separate it in strings with the help of two forks. Set aside.

Cube the tomatoes, peeled and seeded; peel the onions and garlic and chop them finely. Add the beef strings and add salt and pepper.

Place 8 Tbsp. oil in a thick-bottomed pan and fry the mixture for about 15 minutes over medium heat, until the onion is transparent. Set aside.

Cook the rice in 2 cups of water with a tsp. of salt for 20 minutes.

Peel the plantains, cut them in half lengthwise and fry them in 4 Tbsp. oil for 3 minutes at high, until golden. Set aside.

To serve, place the rice in a serving dish, top it with the beef mixture and place the eggs, fried in the rest of the oil, over it.

Surround the rice with caraotas (Recipe #74) and decorate the edges with the plantains.

Other national favorites, such as the entrenched beans, proverbial *sancocho* stews, and the unavoidable *hallacas* (tamales *à la bolivienne,* wrapped in banana leaves), allude to the Colombian kitchen. Banana balls make the difference between the Venezuelan sancocho and that of Spain, as well as from the French *pot-au-feu* and the Argentine *puchero.* Tortoise stew is strictly Venezuelan.

Humboldt (whom, according to the writer Miguel Cané, one must always quote when one uses the trails he took) praises the fish and bananas, which in tropical climes are always preferable to the best foods, he assures us. About 1880 the same Cané, while staying at an inn in Guaira, admitted

Caraotas (Venezuela) #74

INGREDIENTS
(Makes 4 servings)
1 cup black beans
1 onion
1 red pepper
1 green pepper

1 clove garlic
2 Tbsp. olive oil
1 tsp. sugar
1 tsp. cumin
2 quarts water
salt

PREPARATION

Soak the beans in one quart of water for 2 hours. Drain.

Put one quart of water in a thick-bottomed pot, add the beans and cook, covered, for 1½ to 2 hours over medium heat, until tender. Set aside.

Peel and finely chop the peppers, without seeds or membranes, the onion and the garlic. Fry everything in oil for 10 minutes over medium heat; add the sugar, salt, and cumin; mix and add to the beans.

Continue cooking, covered, for another 20 minutes over medium heat.

Serve as garnish for the Pabellón.

NOTE
The beans must be dry and whole; therefore, it is important not to overcook them.

his taste for plantains: "On the table are placed many dishes — salt meat in various forms, beef *à la llanera*, roast, and plantains, fried plantains, roast plantains, cooked plantains, sliced, stuffed, plantains in the soup, plantains in a stew, plantains for dessert." On the farms in the Llanos they prefer beef barbecued on a stick.

In the Andean region the traditional food consists of turnovers, meat roasted with brown sugar (*asado negro*), fried pork, goat's stomach, goat cheese, and local preserves. Tourists explore colonial cities such as old Carora (less well-known than Coro, the first capital of Venezuela), and visit coffee plantations and mountain inns. At the end of the 19th century, coffee from Tachira and Mérida brought prosperity to the villages, as shown by their churches with two towers and three naves, according to writer Mariano Picón Salas. Barquisimeto boasts fine fare and generous wine.

In the 125 fertile miles between there and Caracas, the cordillera's valleys lose their Andean majesty and the coastal valleys become friendly with their stews and little shark-meat turnovers. The Caribbean coast should be explored from port to port, with its tourist complexes, solitary rocky outcrops, and fishing hamlets where the tiny eating-houses smell of fried fish. Another popular tourist destination is Macuro, where America was first recognized as a new continent. When Columbus arrived here, he thought he had found the biblical Eden. At what looks like a green needle on the map, one can detect the aromas of Antillean and Indian cooking, the latter from Trinidad. The name Venezuela, however, comes from a spot

Cachapas *(Venezuela)* #75

INGREDIENTS
(Makes 10)
1 cup corn kernels
1 egg
½ cup whipping cream

¾ cup flour
1 dash salt
1 dash sugar
3 Tbsp. butter

PREPARATION

Grind the corn kernels in a food processor, place them in a bowl and add the egg, the cream, the flour, the salt and the sugar. Mix until creamy and set aside.

Grease a thick-bottomed pan, heat it at medium for 3 minutes, drop 2 Tbsp. of the mixture onto the pan and distribute it to form a disc about ¼" thick and 3 inches in diameter. Fry over medium heat for 3 minutes on each side until golden. Repeat the procedure until you get 10 cachapas. Serve hot.

> NOTE
> In Venezuela cachapas are used instead of bread. They may be spread with different kinds of cheese, rolled over themselves and served as an entrée.
> Arepas are made by the same procedure, only using corn flour, water and salt.

farther west where Vespucio discovered at the entrance to Maracaibo Bay an enormous settlement whose houses rose from the sea as in Venice. These homes on stilts, gaily colored with tiny gardens against a forest backdrop, welcome visitors with fish and cold beer. Venezuelans value their fruit drinks and claim their rum and cocoa are the best in the world.

Finally, Venezuela is as southern and Amazonian as the flowing Orinoco. The few dots on the map represent Indian villages and tourist lodgings built like the native homes (*churiatas*). These unpopulated regions spurred the creation of mythical countries of literature, such as Conan Doyle's Lost World, inspired by the *tepuis,* the world's most ancient tablelands. The traveler who heads inland towards Brazilian Guyana and Manaus has busses and decent feeding stops, which would have delighted the famished seekers of Eldorado.

Craftswoman on a reservation. Ecuador.

Photo: Steve Winter-Black Star

Galapagos
Islands, Ecuador.

*E*cuador takes its name from the earth's longest line of latitude. The Andes cordillera is the backbone of historic, agricultural, and indigenous Ecuador. Half her people live in the valleys and *paramos*; the other half live on the coast where the economic center, Guayaquil, stands.

Highland soups are the ubiquitous *locro* (meat, potato, and cheese), *repe* (green plantains and cheese), hill *guatita* (the coastal tripe dish), and Cuenca's *mote pata* (pork soup traditionally served during Carnival). The coastal dish is rice with a stew of pre-Colombian vegetables and black beans, followed by fish with roast plantains and rice, though ceviches are sometimes served, as are seafood soups such as *biche manabita* and Esmeralda's *pusandao*.

Fanesca (Ecuador) #76

INGREDIENTS
(Makes 8 servings)
1¾ lb. codfish
2 onions
2 cloves garlic
2 zucchinis
2 bay leaves
1 small cabbage

1 small yellow squash
1 tsp. oregano
1 tsp. cumin
4 Tbsp. rice
4 Tbsp. fresh corn
  kernels
4 Tbsp. fresh broad
  beans

4 Tbsp. green peas
4 Tbsp. soft cheese,
  cubed
4 Tbsp. grated
  Parmesan cheese
4 Tbsp. whipping
  cream
4 Tbsp. butter

2 Tbsp. chopped
  peanuts
5 cups milk
3 hardboiled eggs
½ lb. green beans
1 quart water
1 cup hot water
salt and pepper

PREPARATION

Soak the codfish for 10 hours, changing the water frequently to eliminate all the salt.

In a thick-bottomed pot place the codfish and 4 cups of water and cook for 20 minutes over medium heat, until tender. Remove and set the cooking broth aside.

Skin and bone the codfish, cut it in small pieces and set aside.

Finely chop the onions and sauté them in butter, together with the crushed garlic, for 10 minutes over medium heat. Add the oregano, cumin, bay leaves cut in half, salt and pepper, and continue sautéing for 2 minutes.

Add the hot water, the rice, the corn, the cabbage, finely chopped, the broad beans, the green beans cut in halves, the zucchinis, sliced, the green peas, the squash, peeled and diced, the peanuts, the milk and the whipping cream. Stir well, cover and cook for 40 minutes over medium heat.

Finally, add the broth, the codfish and the diced soft cheese and cook for another 5 minutes, until the cheese begins to melt.

Serve hot in individual bowls. Sprinkle with grated Parmesan cheese and top with the chopped hardboiled eggs.

NOTE
Should the fanesca be too thick, it can be thinned by adding hot milk.

Llapingachos *(Ecuador)* #77

INGREDIENTS
(Makes 8 servings)
4 white *chola* potatoes
4 Tbsp. butter

4 Tbsp. lard
2 onions
2 Tbsp. chopped
  parsley

2 cups grated semi-
  hard cheese
4 cups water
salt and pepper

PREPARATION

Peel the potatoes and boil them whole in a quart of water for 20 minutes over medium heat, until tender (*Chola* potatoes are typical and characteristic of Ecuador. Should they be replaced by a different variety, we suggest adding 3 Tbsp. wheat flour to the puree so that the *llapingachos* will not lose their shape when fried). Drain, cool and mash until smooth. Add salt and pepper and set aside. Finely chop the onions, sauté them in butter for 10 minutes over medium heat until translucent and mix them with the mashed potatoes.

Take small portions of the puree and form balls approximately 2 inches in diameter. Make an indentation in their centers, fill them with grated cheese, close the indentation and flatten them between your hands until they are 1¼ inches thick.

Put the llapingachos in the fridge and allow them to cool for 20 minutes.

Fry them in lard for 5 minutes on each side over high heat, until golden.

Serve hot, sprinkled with chopped parsley.

> **NOTE**
> The cheese may be added to the purée instead of being used as a filling.

The lowland Ecuadorian finds the mountains mysteriously attractive, so it is easier to find their plains recipes in the mountains than the other way round. Avocados and sauce made from toasted ground peanuts in soups, stews, and roast meats seem to defy gastronomic frontiers. Between the hills and the sea some indigenous peoples dye their bodies with *achiote*, the great food colorant in Latin American cooking.

In 1534 Spaniards refounded the Inca city of Quito up on the hills along the snow-capped volcanoes. Today it is the great historic center of Latin America, its brown roof-tiles and narrow streets with their antique street lamps seeming to reflect the gentle pace of former times. Quito is surrounded by suburbs with indigenous names like Sangolqui where citizens flock to eat the best *hornado,* the dish of the hills. Otavalo is known for its colorful indigenous market of woven cloths and foods. In 1735 a European scientific mission led by La Condaminé landed in Ecuador's tropics to determine the circumference of the world. Fortunately for us, they also noted the local eating habits. In the event of some foreign nation capturing strategic Guayaquil, they reported, they would not be able to survive without substituting the roasted green plantain for wheat bread. (Ecuador is one of the world's main exporters of plantains and bananas). They also wrote of the use and abuse of cane liquor. In December the founding of the city is celebrated with bullfights and a lot of drinking. Ecuadorians call the last month of the year *beviembre* — roughly "Drinkember."

Squash Cake *(Ecuador)* #78

INGREDIENTS
(Makes 6 servings)
1¼ lb. yellow squash
1 quart water
1 tsp. ground cinnamon
6 Tbsp. sugar
1 Tbsp. butter, melted

6 Tbsp. whipping cream
6 Tbsp. rum
⅔ cup seedless white raisins
2 cups grated semi-hard cheese
2 eggs, beaten
1 Tbsp. butter (for the pan)

PREPARATION

Peel and dice the squash, and cook it in one quart of water for 20 minutes over medium heat, until tender. Remove, drain very well to eliminate as much water as possible, discard the liquid and set the flesh aside.

Once the squash has reached room temperature, mash it until smooth, place it in a thick-bottomed pot, and add the cinnamon, sugar, melted butter and cream. Mix continuously with a wooden spoon and cook for 15 minutes over medium heat, until firm.

Remove from heat and cool.

Once the mixture is cold add the rum, the raisins, the grated cheese and the eggs, beaten. Mix well to blend in all ingredients.

Grease a 10-inch diameter cake pan, 2 inch deep, and pour the mixture into it.

Preheat the oven to medium (350ºF) and bake for 45 minutes until firm and golden.

Remove, cool and unmold. Serve in individual portions.

NOTE
It can be served with cream, lightly whipped with a tsp. of rum.

Corn Locro (Ecuador) #79

INGREDIENTS
(Makes 6 servings)
3 ears of corn
3 cups water
3 Tbsp. *achiote* (saffron) oil
6 potatoes

6 Tbsp. grated semi-hard cheese
6 Tbsp. milk
1 white onion
salt and pepper

PREPARATION

Finely chop the onion and sauté in the achiote oil for 15 minutes over medium heat. Add the ears of corn and the peeled potatoes, both quartered, and continue frying for 5 minutes.

Add the water and cook, covered, for 30 minutes.

Once the potatoes are tender, add the grated cheese and the milk. Add salt and pepper and cook for 10 minutes over medium heat, until the cheese starts melting.

Serve hot in individual bowls.

NOTE
To prepare the achiote oil, mix six Tbsp. of hot vegetable oil with one tsp. achiote seeds; strain, discard the seeds and keep the oil.

The tropical and rainy east is the *País de la Canela* (Cinnamon Country) on colonial maps; indeed, the town of Canelos still exists on the edge of the tropical rainforest. South American cinnamon, which indigenous people call *ishpingo,* did not change the world's culinary habits as Asiatic cinnamon did, but it is used in several recipes. The advance of mixed-race colonization and petroleum exploration is altering the forests, traditional home of numerous indigenous peoples, such as the Jíbaros, famous — or infamous — for their ability to shrink human heads without altering the facial features.

In the streets of Ecuador one can eat corn-on-the-cob and *fritadas* (fried pork with stewed corn) and *verde* (plantain) or *morocho* (sweet corn)

Quimbolitos *(Ecuador)* #80

INGREDIENTS
(Makes 8 servings)

4 Tbsp. seedless white raisins
2 Tbsp. rum
4 Tbsp. butter
4 Tbsp. sugar
2 eggs
4 Tbsp. milk
4 Tbsp. wheat flour
4 tsp. powdered yeast
4 Tbsp. cornstarch
4 Tbsp. grated Parmesan cheese
cotton twine as needed
8 12-in. squares of waxed paper

PREPARATION

Soak the raisins in rum for an hour. Drain and set aside.

Beat the butter at room temperature with the sugar until creamy. Mix the eggs with the milk and add them to the cream, stirring with a wooden spoon. Add the flour, sifted together with the yeast and the cornstarch, and blend in with soft motions.

Finally, add the grated cheese and the raisins. Mix well.

Place three Tbsp. of the mixture in the center of each wax paper square, fold the edges up to hold the filling and tie with a piece of twine.

Steam for 40 minutes over medium heat. Remove, take the paper wraps off and serve hot.

NOTE
In Ecuador the wax paper is replaced by leaves of achira, a traditional plant with large leaves and showy flowers.

turnovers. Lemons with salt help combat dehydration. One should try *paila* ice cream and figs in syrup with soft cheese. A sit-down meal leans heavily on the soup course (trotter broth or locro), *seco de chivo* (mutton with the ever-present helping of rice — one of the better known Ecuadorian dishes), and fruit. In wealthier homes, cooks tend to prepare traditional indigenous and local dishes — fruited corn mush, *choclantadas* (sweet corn stuffed with cheese Ecuadorian-style), *quimbolitos, llapinga-chos,* and *pristiños.* From grandmothers' recipes comes *fanesca* (a Lenten stew of colorful beans and fish) accompanied by a mulberry drink, *colada morada.*

Pristiños *(Ecuador)* #81

INGREDIENTS
(Makes 8 servings)

2½ cups wheat flour
¾ cup butter
½ lb. yellow squash
4 Tbsp. grated
Parmesan cheese

8 Tbsp. lard
8 tsp. brown sugar
2 cups water
1 tsp. powdered yeast
1 tsp. salt

PREPARATION

Peel and dice the squash and cook it in 2 cups of water for 20 minutes over medium heat, until soft. Remove, drain, and mash until smooth. Set aside.

Sift the flour with the salt and the yeast; mix it with the grated cheese, the mashed squash and the butter at room temperature.

Pour the mixture onto a floured table top and roll to a thickness of approximately ¾ inch. Cut in 1 x 2-inch strips and join the ends forming rings.

Fry the strips in lard for 5 minutes at high until golden. Remove and drain on paper towels.

Serve sprinkled with brown sugar.

NOTE
The purée must be firm so that the rings will not crumble when fried.

Photo: Laurent Giraudou-Ag. Anzenberger

Traditional hat workshop, Ecuador.

Photo: Gerard Sioen/Ag. Anzenberger

Lake Titicaca,
Bolivia.

*B*olivia is the Inca's *Collasuyu,* the Spanish conquistadors' *Collao* (the country of the Collas and Aymaras), and *Alto Perú* (Upper Peru) of viceregal history. An inland country, it lost its outlet to the sea that so benefits other Andean countries. A museum in La Paz is dedicated to recalling that tragic event, which deprives Bolivia, amongst other things, of its shellfish and ceviches.

Bolivia's sea is Lake Titicaca, where reed boats sail as in lower Mesopotamia, and where fish for the tables of La Paz is caught. On its shores is the archaeological sanctuary of Tihuanaku, the ancient capital of the Aymara culture that enormously influenced the Inca empire.

Sopaipillas Cochabambinas (Bolivia) #82

INGREDIENTS
(Makes 24)
1 lb. pumpkin
1 lb. wheat flour

4 Tbsp. butter
1 Tbsp. sugar
salt
½ tsp. anise seeds

½ tsp. baking soda
2 cups water
honey as needed
vegetable oil as needed

PREPARATION

Peel the pumpkin, dice it and cook it in 2 cups of water for 20 minutes over medium heat. Remove, drain and process.

Place the pumpkin in a bowl and mix it with the flour, salt, sugar, hot melted butter, anise and baking soda. Knead well until smooth.

Roll the dough with a rolling pin to ⅛-inch thickness, and cut with a 2-inch cookie cutter. Prick each disc with a fork and fry them in very hot oil for 5 minutes until golden.

Serve the warm sopaipillas sprinkled with honey.

NOTE
Add a little of the pumpkin cooking water to make the dough more yellow.

To the east of Cuzco *humitas, chuños,* and *chichas* are cross-border mockeries of territoriality; here the Andes spread to enclose the high plateau where La Paz, Oruro, and Potosí lie. It is the region where the Aymara language is most widely spoken and where the people wear vibrantly colored clothing. The temperate valleys of Cochabamba, Chuquisaca, and Tarija descend to the tropical plains, forested in the humid north where maps show a total lack of roads but rivers head for the Amazon, and the green eastern savannahs.

In terms of food, the heights are dominated by soups with beef (*chairo*), pork (*fricassee*), or chicken (*chacao*) accompanied by potatoes, peppers,

Chicken K'oko *(Bolivia)* #83

INGREDIENTS
(Makes 8 servings)
1 4½-lb. chicken
3 onions
6 locoto peppers
1 yellow pepper

2 Tbsp. oregano
4 Tbsp. chopped parsley
¼ lb. pitted black olives
¼ lb. pitted prunes
4 cups red wine
4 cups water

2 cups malt beer
6 Tbsp. vegetable oil
salt and pepper

Cut the onions in thin strips and sauté them in the oil for 10 minutes over medium heat, until translucent. Add the yellow pepper, quartered, without seeds or membranes, the oregano, and two Tbsp. of parsley and continue cooking for 10 minutes. Add salt and pepper; add the water, wine, malt and locoto peppers, without seeds or membranes, cut in thin strips. Cover and cook for 20 minutes over medium heat.

Cut the chicken in 8 pieces, add to the mixture and continue cooking for 40 minutes until the meat is tender.

Remove from the heat and add the pitted prunes and olives cut in halves.

Serve hot in individual bowls, sprinkled with the remaining chopped parsley.

> **NOTE**
> If you prefer the flavor of beer, change the beer-wine ratio —
> 4 cups of beer to 2 cups of wine.

---

corn on the cob, and vegetables, and the very popular *laguas* of corn, quinoa, or ground peanuts. *Locote* is the fiery Bolivian pepper used in chicken *picantes* (known as far south as Salta in Argentina but tamed to please the southern palate), beef stews (*saice* and *sajta*), and *locro,* "in which they pour so much hot pepper that the Indians and even some Spaniards cannot eat it without shedding tears," according to Father Bernabé Cobo, one of the chroniclers more attuned to cordilleran tastes. When Andean locro (jerked beef and cracked corn) reaches the plains it is varied with chicken, plantains, and rice. There is even a locro *carretero* for travelers, a simplified recipe.

Silpancho is the national breaded meat, served with potatoes in the mountains or fried plantains on the plains. Cheese and manioc are combined in *cuñapes*, *masacos* (recommended as an accompaniment to coffee) and *zonzos cruceños*. Sausages from Chuquisaca and lamb from Oruro (roasted in their hide or basted) have made names for themselves, as has the soft cheese from Tarija, sweets from Potosí, and Cochabamba's *sopaipillas* (fried tortillas of flour and pumpkin, like those from Chile) spread with *chancana* syrup. In the valleys of Tarija and Cochabamba wine is produced, though the national drink is beer, especially the kind from La Paz.

Breakfast for wealthy Bolivians consists of fruit juices, lots of coffee, toast, and biscuits. The mid-afternoon snack is served with *queque* (sponge cake with cane syrup). The main meal is lunch. In pensions and taverns there are always one or two daily specials and it is a rare occasion when empanadas are not offered. Potatoes, meat, and grains are the main ingredients in stews. By contrast, the Aymara shepherd's diet is very austere.

Ancucus Potosinos (Bolivia) #84

INGREDIENTS
(Makes 24)
1 lb. chancaca (brown sugar)

½ cup water
grated rind of one lemon
2 cups shelled peanuts

PREPARATION

In a thick-bottomed saucepan place the chancaca, the water and the lemon rind and cook for 20 minutes over medium heat, until deep golden.

Remove, pour half of the caramel on a marble surface, spread the shelled peanuts over it and cover with the remaining caramel.

Allow to cool slightly and cut in 1-inch squares.

NOTE
Brush the marble surface with vegetable oil to prevent the caramel from sticking to it.

He undertakes the droving of llamas over long distances with rations of *chuño* (dried potatoes) and coca leaves which, according to Acosta, "puts strength and encouragement into the Indian as one can notice effects which are not attributable to the imagination; with a fistful of coca he can walk for two days without eating."

Bolivia has colonial cities (Sucre, Cochabamba, Potosí), ancient churches and convents, colorful native folk festivals such as the Diabladas de Oruro, motley street markets, and train stops where foods are paid for with rations of adventure. In San José de Chiquitos smoking stoves compensate for the chronic delay of the train by offering the pure pleasure of a trackside snack and a refreshing drink of cinnamon and tamarind. If one has time the Chiquitos Mission is worth a visit. It spreads over seven scattered plains villages that outlasted the Jesuits, with wooden buildings and multicolored chapels roofed in the country style.

Recipe Glossary (Andean Region)

BOLIVIA

ANCUCUS: nougat of peanuts or almonds and honey.

CHANCACA: brown sugar.

LOCOTO PEPPERS: typical Bolivian hot peppers.

SOPAIPILLAS: fritters.

COLOMBIA

AJIACO: meat and vegetable soup or stew.

AGUACATE: avocado.

CREOLE PEPPER: small, sweet pepper.

HOT PEPPER: small green pepper

ALMOJÁBANAS: yellow or white corn, separated from the chaff and soaked to soften it.

AREPA: round, flat cornbread.

GUASCA: typical aromatic herb. May be replaced by sweet basil.

HOGAO OR HOGO: sautéed tomato and onion.

CHALA: corn husk.

LARD: may be replaced by corn or olive oil.

CREOLE POTATO: yellow potato, young potato.

PASTUSA POTATO: black potato.

SABANERA POTATO: white potato.

PLÁTANO: plantain.

ECUADOR

ACHIOTE: achiote seeds, may be replaced by saffron.

CACAHUETES: peanuts.

LARD: may be replaced by corn or olive oil.

LOCRO: thick stew of cracked corn, meats, pumpking, potatoes, etc.

PERU

CEBICHE, CEVICHE: macerated fish eaten raw.

CHUPE: fish or meat stews.

PANCA PEPPER: Large, purple-colored, sun-dried pepper. Ground panca pepper may be replaced by paprika.

ROCOTO PEPPER: hot pepper shaped like a pimento but smaller.

CAMOTE: sweet potato.

NATILLAS: cream custard.

EVAPORATED MILK: natural whole milk concentrated to half its initial state. May be replaced by regular milk.

YELLOW POTATO: a typical variety of potato. It may be replaced by a common potato.

HUAYRO POTATO: a pink-colored, sandy kind of potato.

DRY POTATO: potato dehydrated by exposure to the very low temperatures of the Peruvian Andes. They are sold crushed.

TOMASA POTATO: a typical variety, may be replaced by white potato.

PLÁTANO: plantain.

VENEZUELA

CARAOTAS: beans.

CONO SUR

Glaciar Perito Moreno, Santa Cruz. Argentina.   Photo: Jorge Luis Campos

And as soon as we asked for it they brought hens, geese, sheep, ostriches, venison and other victuals until we were sated.

—Ulrico Schmidel

Argentina, Chile, Uruguay, and Paraguay close the map of South America at its southernmost tip. The guidebooks confirm Argentina and Uruguay as countries of good beef; Chile as the paradise of seafood. The geography of bananas and manioc ends in Paraguay. Strong cultural and gastronomical vestiges — such as *mate,* barbecue, and wine — tie the south of Brazil to the geographic and historical environment of the gaucho world.

Situated on the periphery of the indigenous empires of potatoes and corn, the cuisine of the Cono Sur, the southern half of South America, had its origins in the colonial tradition but did not reach maturity until it received the contributions of immigration (1860–1915), which changed the history of the region. Immigration consolidated the national development of the recently liberated countries, saved waves of Europeans from starvation, and diversified the colonial menu. Before, during the Hispanic colonial and post-colonial period, the natives ate dishes of Creole inspiration with varying degrees of African or indigenous influence. After, an immigrant cuisine grew and prospered, with European recipes enhanced by the abundant beef of the region. Areas with a marked folk tradition, such as the Chilean Great North, the Argentine Northwest, the Chiloé Island region, and the Guarani lands, are considered sanctuaries of regional and even national cooking.

The Cono Sur is a subcontinent of 1.81 million square miles, the equivalent of half the area of China. It contains the widest plains and the driest deserts. Only the Cordillera of the Andes limits the landscape, separating the realm of beef spread on generous grills to the east from the fish and seafood stews that flourish in the kitchens on the Pacific.

Coming from Peru, Arica inaugurates the splendid markets with the cries of the fresh fish vendors and the scent of seafood fritters that will stay with the traveler who continues south with the Chilean geography. The precarious Bolivian roads will take tourists to the Argentine Northwest, whose valleys and cordilleras preserve the last vestiges of the folk culture of the Alto Peru.

Photo: Carlos Mordo

Jesuit ruins,
Trinidad,
Paraguay.

Deeper south, locros and humitas (corn-based dishes) become scarcer; they reappear now and again in a few urban restaurants that keep the taste for regional gastronomy alive. Buenos Aires is the entrance to the Pampean granary, a plain without horizon or borders that becomes an arid steppe and finally reaches Patagonia, mythical and distant, exciting the imagination of travelers with its vast estancias.

CHILE

Chile — an enigmatic country, according to poet Pablo Neruda — is curious even to look at on a map. A single main road runs through landscapes of rain and snow, of salt mines and deserts where it hasn't rained for over a century. This is the Carretera Central (Central Road), probably so called because it rarely reaches the coastline, or maybe because it goes through the capital, Santiago, which was not founded by the sea but at the foot of the Andes, almost as far from Arica as from the Strait of Magellan.

The national cuisine is basically marine. Chileans, paraphrasing Mirabeau, say that the sea is a plain that cultivates itself. Writer Benjamin Subercaseaux, in his book *Tierra de océano* (*Land of Ocean*), refers to fishermen as "the sea's peasants." Actually, Chile is a 2,485-mile-long fish market. Even when the sea is far away — though the map confirms that it is never too far away — the fish can be smelled in the markets, which encompass, perhaps better than in any other country in the region, the convergence of national flavors.

The most highly prized fish is the king clip, prepared in thick slices with onions and potatoes in a thin stew that Neruda's verses and popular taste have made the patriotic symbol of Chilean cuisine. Experts affirm that it is one of the best bouillabaisses in the world.

Shellfish is no less prized: the very Chilean locos, scallops, pink clams, hard clams, cholgas, piures, and mussels combine in succulent *mariscales,* next to vieiras, oysters, lobster, shrimp, and huge sea urchins. These delicacies are prepared raw or cooked in sauces, breaded, floured, baked, fried with garlic (*pilpil*), barbecued, grilled, stuffed, in soups, and in *chupes* (a type of stew). They are usually accompanied by *sopaipillas,* the Chilean version of the fritter; as spongy as they are delicious, they are a must at lunch, spread with *pebre* (chimichurri with coriander) or jams and preserves at *onces* time (tea time).

Chiloé National Park, Chile.

Pebre (Chile) #85

INGREDIENTS
(Makes 4 servings)
2 tomatoes
2 onions

2 green peppers
4 cloves garlic
4 Tbsp. olive oil
juice of one lemon

4 Tbsp. finely chopped
  fresh coriander
salt and pepper

PREPARATION

Dice the tomatoes, peeled and seeded.

Finely chop the onions and dice the peppers, without seeds or membranes, in cubes of the same size as those of the tomatoes.

Finely mince the garlic, mix with the rest of the vegetables and set aside.

Mix the olive oil, the lemon juice and the finely chopped coriander in a bowl. Add salt and pepper to taste and beat until homogeneous; add to the vegetables and mix.

This sauce is great for fish, shellfish and all kinds of meats.

NOTE
If you wish to temper the flavor of the onions, once chopped, mix them with one Tbsp. of sugar and another of salt. Allow to rest for 10 minutes and wash with cold water before adding the remaining ingredients.

From Arica to Punta Arenas, Creole cuisine is committed to American staples like corn (present in the ubiquitous corn pie) and beans, cooked and seasoned in the Chilean fashion — *porotos granados* (beans with vegetables) and *porotos con rienda* (beans with "reins," an allusion to the spaghetti that arrived with Italian immigration).

The meridian of the Chilean markets passes through Arica, Chillán, Concepción, Temuco, Valdivia, Puerto Montt, Castro. Moved by curiosity and appetite, visitors will check out many more. If there is no time to visit them all, at least they should visit the Mercado Central de Santiago, in the ancient part of the city. This market is as famous for its *cocinerías* (street kitchens) as for its huge iron top, prefabricated in England and traditionally attributed to Gustave Eiffel.

From Santiago, the true starting point of national gastronomy, some of the gastronomic routes to good eating fan out, forcing travelers to stop here

Tomaticán *(Chile) #86*

INGREDIENTS
(Makes 6 servings)
1 ½-lb. beef rump
10 tomatoes

3 potatoes
3 ears of corn
3 cloves garlic
3 hardboiled eggs

1 onion
1 green pepper
1 Tbsp. chopped
  parsley

1 Tbsp. oregano
6 Tbsp. olive oil
salt and pepper

PREPARATION

Cube the beef and brown it in oil together with the onion and the garlic, finely chopped, for 10 minutes over medium heat.

Add the potatoes, peeled and quartered, the tomatoes, peeled, seeded and cubed, the green pepper, without seeds or membranes, diced, the parsley and the oregano. Add salt and pepper and cook for 20 minutes over medium heat, until the meat is tender.

Separate the grains of corn from the cobs, add them to the pot and continue cooking for 10 minutes.

Serve sprinkled with chopped hardboiled egg.

NOTE
Tenderize the meat by soaking it in hot milk for an hour.

Photo: Explorer

Parinacota
volcano, Chile.

and there to try empanadas and sausages, *guañacas* and pork ribs, regional wines and country dishes that cause a healthy delay. Visitors must ven-
ture on the road to Curicó and Talca, the capitals of *plateadas* (pot roast
with spicy mashed potatoes); or else along the road to steep Valparaíso,
going through the confectioneries of Curacaví — famous for its *manjar
blanco* (milk jam) — finally reaching the seafood places in the seaside
resort of Pichilemu or on Isla Negra, where the home of Pablo Neruda
has been turned into a museum.

The Biobío River was the historical and even judicial border between
Spain and Araucania. The Araucanos or Mapuches constitute the main

Hallullas (Chile) #87

INGREDIENTS
(Makes 36)
2 tsp. sugar
4 tsp. yeast

1½ lb. + 1 tsp. wheat flour
2 cups water
2 Tbsp. powdered milk
1 Tbsp. salt

2 Tbsp. butter
2 egg yolks
1 Tbsp. butter (for the mold)

PREPARATION

Dissolve the sugar, the yeast and one tsp. of flour in half a cup of lukewarm water; allow to ferment for 15 minutes and set aside.

Mix the wheat flour with the powdered milk and the salt. Pour on the table top forming a crown, place the fermented yeast mixture in the center and gradually add the remaining water and the melted butter at room temperature. Knead until smooth, cover with a cheesecloth and allow to rest for 35 minutes.

Roll the dough with a rolling pin to ¼-inch thickness and cut with a 2½ to 3-inch diameter pastry cutter. Prick the discs with a fork and allow them to rise again for 30 minutes.

Place the hallullas on a buttered cookie sheet and paint them with the egg yolks, beaten.

Preheat the oven to high (400°F) and bake for 10 minutes, until golden.

Serve warm.

NOTE
To make it easier to paint the hallullas, thin the egg yolks with a Tbsp. cold water.

indigenous population of Chile, with their own customs, religion, language, and social organization. Long before the German farmers and carpenters of Valdivia imposed the Alpine style of Bariloche (towards 1895), the Araucanos were already cooking *curantos* and making *piñon* flour (from the seeds of the *pehuén,* a prehistoric conifer of the southern woods).

The island of Chiloé attracts tourists with its natural beauty, its wooden houses, chapels, and lake dwellings, its mythology and its folk traditions. Its markets confirm the abundance of terrestrial and maritime foods that sustain native cooking, Creole and sea-based, considered the most picturesque and regional of Chile. In this small land of fishermen, farmers, and

Leche Nevada (Chile) #88

INGREDIENTS
(Makes 6 servings)
4 cups milk
4 eggs
6 Tbsp. cold milk

3 Tbsp. warm milk
2 Tbsp. cornstarch
1 cup sugar
1 tsp. vanilla extract

Separate the egg whites from the yolks and beat them until they form stiff peaks. Set aside.

In a thick-bottomed pot, heat the four cups of milk, the sugar and the vanilla extract for 15 minutes over medium heat.

Drop the egg whites by spoonfuls into the boiling milk, forming puffs and pouring some of the boiling milk over them with a spoon so that they will cook. Remove them and place them on a serving dish. Set the milk aside.

Dissolve the cornstarch in cold milk, gradually add the hot milk set aside, stirring constantly with a wooden spoon, and boil for 5 minutes over medium heat.

Place the egg yolks in a bowl, add 3 Tbsp. warm milk to thin them, mix and add them to the mixture to form a cream. Pour it over the puffs and cool in the fridge for 3 hours.

> **NOTE**
> Add a tsp. of cornstarch to the egg whites to make them firmer.

---

carpenters, shellfish and abundant *curantos* set the pace. The islanders feed on their own wild potatoes which, according to some, could be even more ancient than those of Peru.

Between the seafood stews and southern barbecues is the characteristic curanto, which consists in gathering a variety of shellfish, fish, chicken, and vegetables and cooking them slowly between layers of stones heated in a wood fire and buried in a pit. Curanto is served with *milcaos* and *chapaleles* (potato croquettes) and is eaten outdoors (Chile, according to Darwin, is an extraordinary country for cooking outdoors). It has spread from the island of Chiloé to Puerto Montt, where travelers will probably taste it for the first time, in its crock pot version (*pulmay*), less authentic than in its natural container, the earth, which is now less frequently used. Migrants from Chiloé and Puerto Montt carried with them the custom of the pulmay to the Magellanic region.

South of Araucania, the Cordillera cuts the map into islands and small bays that announce the Patagonian region. Among remote estancias and forgotten hamlets, through glaciers and wooded fjords, the cyclopean

Corn Pie *(Chile)* #89

INGREDIENTS
(Makes 6 servings)

FIRST STEP
6 pieces of chicken
1 carrot, finely chopped
1 onion, finely chopped
3 Tbsp. olive oil
1 cup dry white wine
salt and pepper

SECOND STEP
2 Tbsp. olive oil
1 Tbsp. butter
1 lb. ground beef
½ tsp. cumin
½ Tbsp. paprika
½ tsp. oregano
salt and pepper
1 cup beef broth

THIRD STEP
2 Tbsp. butter
kernels of 6 ears of
   corn
2 Tbsp. milk
1 tsp. sugar
1 Tbsp. finely chopped
   fresh basil
salt and pepper

OTHER
6 tsp. chopped black
   olives
6 tsp. seedless white
   raisins
2 hardboiled eggs
6 Tbsp. sugar

Torres del Paine national park, Chile.

Photo: Panoramic Images

FIRST STEP

Brown the pieces of chicken in 3 Tbsp. of oil for 20 minutes over medium heat, turning them so that they will brown evenly.

Add the onion and the carrot, finely chopped, add salt and pepper, add the wine and allow to concentrate for 20 minutes, until the chicken is tender. Remove from heat and set aside.

SECOND STEP

In a thick-bottomed pan, heat the oil and 1 Tbsp. butter for 5 minutes over low heat. Add the ground beef and brown for 15 minutes, stirring constantly with a wooden spoon.

Add the cumin, the paprika and the oregano. Add salt and pepper, add the broth and cook for 20 minutes, until the meat is tender. Remove from heat and set aside.

THIRD STEP

In a thick-bottomed pan, heat the butter for 5 minutes over medium heat; add the ground kernels of corn and cook for 15 minutes, stirring constantly with a wooden spoon until the mixture thickens. Add salt and pepper, add the sugar and the milk, mix, add the basil, turn off the heat and cool. Set aside.

In individual crock bowls, place a portion of the ground beef mixture, a tsp. of raisins, one of olives and one of chopped hardboiled egg.

Add the chicken, cover with the corn mixture, sprinkle with a tsp. of sugar and heat in the oven for 20 minutes at medium, until the sugar is slightly golden.

Remove and serve hot.

Shellfish Stew *(Chile)* #90

INGREDIENTS
(Makes 6 servings)
1 lb. mussels
1 lb. clams
1 lb. shrimp
1 lb. king clip
1 onion
1 clove garlic

1 tomato
2 bay leaves, halved
1 tsp. Merquén or
   regular crushed red
   pepper
1 tsp. oregano
4 Tbsp. olive oil
1 cup dry white wine

salt and pepper
1 quart fish broth
1 tsp. chopped
   coriander

FISH BROTH
6 cups water
1 leek

1 carrot
1 celery stalk
Head, backbone and
   tail of a king clip
1 bay leaf
1 tsp. salt

PREPARATION

Wash the mussels, the clams, the shrimp and the king clip in abundant water. If they are in their shells, it is advisable to soak them in cold water with salt for 10 minutes so that they will release the sand they might have.

Wash the king clip, keeping the head, backbone and tail of the fish for the broth. Set aside.

Finely chop the onion and the garlic, dice the tomato, peeled and seeded, and fry everything in the oil, together with the bay leaf halves, the merquén and the oregano, for 10 minutes over medium heat. Stir often so that the mixture will cook evenly.

Add salt and pepper and the wine, allowing the alcohol to evaporate for 5 minutes. Add the fish broth and heat over medium heat until it starts to boil. Add the king clip, cut in medium pieces, the clams, the mussels and the shrimp and cook for 20 minutes over medium heat until the shellfish open.

Serve hot in individual bowls and sprinkle with chopped coriander.

FISH BROTH
Boil the vegetables, cut in pieces, the bay leaf, the salt and the tail, backbone and head of the king clip for an hour over medium heat.

Remove and strain.

Bean Stew *(Chile)* #91

INGREDIENTS
(Makes 6 servings)
1¼ lb. beans
1¼ lb. squash

3 Tbsp. corn kernels
3 tomatoes
3 Tbsp. olive oil
1 onion

2 Tbsp. paprika
1 tsp. oregano
4 cups water
salt and pepper

PREPARATION

Wash the beans and cook them in a quart of water for 2 hours over medium heat, until tender, add a tsp. of salt at the end of the cooking time. Drain and keep both the beans and the broth separately.

Finely chop the onion and sauté it in the oil with the paprika for 10 minutes over medium heat.

Add the tomatoes, peeled, seeded and cubed, and the oregano. Add salt and pepper and continue simmering for 10 minutes until the sauce becomes creamy. Set aside.

Place the beans in a thick-bottomed pot, add the squash, cubed, the sauce, the kernels of corn and the bean broth. Cover and simmer for 25 to 30 minutes, until the squash is tender.

Serve hot in individual bowls.

> **NOTE**
> If the beans are dry, soak them for 4 hours and boil without salt for 2 hours, adding salt at the end of the cooking time. If the beans are fresh, simmer them, covered, for 40 minutes.

Carretera Austral (Southern Road) opens the way to the Last Frontier in search of Punta Arenas. This southern capital was founded on the site of the ancient *Puerto Hambre* (Port Hunger), a disquieting colonial name that has left aside the misfortunes of navigation to pay homage to the delicious Magellanic lambs and king crabs.

As we move from Santiago to the Great North, brotherhoods, sister-hoods, and pilgrimages in honor of the Virgin become more frequent (Co-piapó, La Tirana, Andacollo), wines become scarcer, and the cebiches, pep-pers, and other spicy dressings that mark Peruvian cooking begin to appear. The desert of Atacama is an area of Aymara folk tradition of the *altiplano* (plateau). Bread-based foods, like the *calatanta* — baked between hot stones traditionally and eaten at funerary banquets — and ceremonial

Pulmay (Chile) #92

INGREDIENTS
(Makes 6 servings)
2 lb. clams
2 lb. mussels
1 4½-lb. chicken

2 onions
2 heads of garlic
6 cups dry white wine
6 sausages
1 tsp. pepper

salt

GARNISH
3 potatoes

Wash the clams and mussels with abundant cold water to eliminate the grit and foreign matter adhered to them. Set aside.

Cut the chicken in six pieces, place them in a thick-bottomed pot and add the wine and the sausages, whole or halved. Cook, uncovered, for 20 minutes over medium heat.

Add the onions, quartered, the heads of garlic, unpeeled, cleaned and whole, the mussels, the clams and the pepper. Add salt and continue cooking for 20 minutes, until the mussels open.

Remove and discard the heads of garlic.

Serve hot, with a garnish of boiled potatoes.

NOTE
It is important to discard any mussels and clams that do not open when cooked.

drinks such as the *pusitunca,* an alcoholic beverage made of corn, honoring Pachamama — are in style in this region. The *guatia,* the northern version of the curanto, gathers everyone around it. The tourist capital of the Chilean Puna is San Pedro de Atacama, where natural thermal springs and geysers can be found.

The Norte Chico (Small North) displays its beauty on the beaches of Coquimbo and La Serena and in the diaphanous heavens of the valley of the Elqui River, where the stars seem to be closer to the earth. Poet Gabriela Mistral, a valley native, calls it *cielo máximo* (maximum sky), and the miners of Coquimbo give it the name *cielo macho* (macho sky). This is why it boasts the highest concentration of telescopes in the world. The Elqui Valley is also the valley of *pisco,* a grape rum drunk with lemon and the juice of the delicious papaya from La Serena.

Pisco sour is the welcoming aperitif offered to foreigners as a certificate of Chilean-ness. The term *sour* (which is not Chilean but English) marks the distance from the city of Pisco, where the famous Peruvian rum is made. Even those who have not tasted pisco consider the Elqui Valley the energy center of the planet.

ARGENTINA

*I*n the perpetually fragmented world of images, Argentina is, above all, the country of the pampas. Travelers do not fall in love at first sight with this extremely green, apparently monotonous plain. For visitors who are short on time, the pampas are an obstacle to be conquered before quickly reaching those relevant edges of the map that have brought them from afar: the Patagonian lakes and glaciers, the cordilleras of Cuyo, the sierras of Cordoba, the northern valleys and gorges, the tropical forests and waterfalls, the marine fauna of the end of the world.

Argentina is a country with diverse climates and landscapes. This is not the typical variety of the Andean countries — presented in tight climatic layers — but a southern vastness, as great as the distance between Stockholm and Cairo. In spite of this advantageous position in the continental share of assets and the quality of the food production, Argentina does not show the complexity that characterizes the Andean, Mexican, or Brazilian markets.

The Argentine gastronomic landscape is dominated by meats and salads, pasta and French fries, wines and wheat bread, *mate* and *dulce de leche*. If we understand national food as that which can be found everywhere at reasonable prices, then the Argentine national dishes are chicken, *milanesas* (breaded veal filets), roast meat, ravioli, and pizza. Empanadas are still the main form of culinary identification among the provinces, although no recipe is definitive regarding ingredients, which depend on the cook, the taste of the clients, and the local produce.

When true natives have been away from their land, they come home thinking about steak, which their appetite identifies as the symbol of their country. *Asado* (barbecued beef) was the main staple of the pampas and of their nomadic gauchos. In the countryside the meat was barbecued in its hide on a spit and diners ate standing around the spit. Later, the improvement of pastures and cattle and the appearance of refrigeration made the suburban weekend *asadito* possible. This was the origin of the barbecue grill and the *quincho,* a thatch-covered area of the backyard. According to the purest theory of role division in barbecued and raw foods of the

Photo: Jorge Luis Campos

Buenos Aires, Argentina.

pampas, the man barbecues and the woman prepares the salads (lettuce, tomato, radish) and dessert (fruit salad, ice cream), all of them modern additions, since the native Creole ate with hard biscuits and *mate*.

Meats can be barbecued horizontally (the classic *parrillada con achuras*) or vertically (on a spit). As the diners wait for the *choripán* (sausage sandwich) that will open the barbecue, they sample a Creole empanada and sip their first glass of Argentine red wine. As they receive their plate, they must express their preference for well done, medium, or rare meat. The most popular cuts are flank steak and short ribs, but the restaurants also offer sirloin and porterhouse steak and grilled Provolone cheese (*provoletta*). Visitors may eat asado at barbecue restaurants (*parrilladas*), at the homes of Argentine friends, or at tourist estancias. The favorite meats

Creole Empanadas *(Argentina) #93*

INGREDIENTS
(Makes 24)
DOUGH
2 lb. flour
11 oz. high-quality beef
   fat
1 cup lukewarm water

1 Tbsp. paprika
salt

FILLING
1 lb. chuck
5 oz. beef fat
1 lb. green onions

2 tomatoes
1 red pepper
2 carrots
2 hardboiled eggs
¼ lb. seedless black
   raisins

¼ lb. green olives,
   pitted
1 tsp. cumin
1 Tbsp. paprika
salt and pepper

PREPARATION

Place the flour on the table forming a well; pour the lukewarm, melted beef fat in the middle, add the paprika, the salt, and gradually add the water as you mix the ingredients with your hands until you get a smooth ball.

Knead for 10 minutes until the dough no longer sticks to your hands, and let it rest in a warm place, covered with a cheesecloth, for 30 minutes.

Roll the dough with a rolling pin to ⅕-inch thickness and cut 4-in. discs with a cutter. Sprinkle the discs with a little flour so that they do not stick to each other and set aside.

FILLING

Finely chop the green onion and fry it in the beef fat 5 minutes over medium heat. Add the carrots, peeled and thinly sliced, the paprika, the tomatoes and the red pepper, both seeded and chopped. Continue cooking for 10 minutes. Add the chuck, finely diced, the salt, the pepper and the cumin, and continue cooking for 5 minutes until the meat is browned.

Remove from heat, add the pitted olives, the hardboiled eggs, chopped, and the raisins. Allow to chill in the fridge.

MAKING THE EMPANADAS

Place two Tbsp. of filling in the center of each disc, moisten the edges with water at room temperature, fold one half of the disc over the other and press the edges together. Fold the edge over itself by twisting it at regular intervals to form a cord and make sure the filling does not come out.

Place the empanadas on a greased cookie sheet, brush them with beaten egg, and bake in hot oven for 10 to 15 minutes until golden.

NOTE
If you like a juicier filling, add a boiled potato, peeled and diced.

Cliff at Valdes
Peninsula,
Chubut,
Argentina.

vary from region to region: beef and pork in the pampas, kid at the sierras, the pre-cordillera, and Santiago del Estero, lamb in Patagonia, fish along the river, and chicken all over the country.

In the times of the May Revolution, while the gaucho barbecued in the countryside, stews ruled in the city. The Spanish-Creole cuisine inaugurated boiled meats. The most popular dishes were *puchero,* repeated through the week with abundance or scarcity, and *carbonada.* The indigenous contribution to the stew was *locro,* with varying versions and aspirations. Only the black slaves — memory of whom was erased from the pampas — took advantage of the entrails that the Creoles disdained. Thus *mondongo* (tripe) was born, which the restaurants insist on calling *a la española* (Spanish style), and *chanfaina,* kid's entrails scrambled in the blood of the freshly slaughtered animal. *Chanfaina* was better appreciated in the times of Independence. It is related to Cuban *friche* and Jorge Amado's *sarapatel* from Bahia.

Carbonada *(Argentina) #94*

INGREDIENTS
(Makes 6 servings)
1 9- to 11-lb. whole
   Creole pumpkin
3 ears of corn

2 tomatoes
1 onion
1 red pepper
1 green pepper
1 lb. veal chuck

½ cup white wine
4 Tbsp. milk
2 Tbsp. sugar
2 Tbsp. butter
2 cups rice

6 Tbsp. olive oil
2 cups vegetable broth
salt and pepper

PREPARATION

Wash the pumpkin well and cut the top to form a lid. Scoop out the seeds. Brush it inside with melted butter, sprinkle with sugar and pour in the milk. Cover it with the lid, put it on an oven pan and bake it for 1¼ hour at medium (350°F) until tender. Set aside.

Sauté the rice in 4 Tbsp. of oil for 10 minutes over medium heat, stirring constantly with a wooden spoon. Set aside.

Cut the ears of corn in halves or in thick slices and boil them in the broth for 10 minutes. Set aside.

Finely chop the onion and the peppers, without seeds or membranes, and fry them in the remaining oil for 10 minutes. Add the chuck, cubed, and the tomatoes, peeled, seeded and diced; add salt and pepper and cook for 20 minutes over medium heat. Add the wine, the rice and the ears of corn, together with the broth, and continue cooking for 10 minutes.

Stuff the pumpkin with the mixture, cover it and heat it in medium oven for 15 or 20 minutes.

Place it on a serving dish and take it to the table. Each guest can then help himself to a piece of the pulp and some stuffing.

NOTE
To help the pumpkin cook evenly, prick the inside with a fork so that the milk can get into the pulp.

Matambre Cooked in Milk (Argentina) #95

INGREDIENTS
(Makes 6 servings)
1 3-lb. piece of plate
1 onion

1 red pepper
3 cloves garlic
3 carrots
3 hardboiled eggs

2 Tbsp. chopped parsley
2 Tbsp. white vinegar
4 cups milk
salt and pepper

Mix the crushed garlic with the parsley and the vinegar. Add salt and pepper and set aside.

Place the plate on the tabletop with the fat part up, cover it with the garlic and parsley and marinate in the fridge for 3 hours.

Finely chop the onion and the pepper, without seeds or membranes, mix them with the peeled, grated carrots and distribute the mixture evenly over the plate. Place the whole hardboiled eggs alongside, roll the plate over itself forming a cylinder and tie it with some twine. Place it in a deep oven pan, pour the milk over it and roast at medium (350°F) for an hour, until tender. Add more milk if necessary.

Remove, place the matambre between two wooden boards and press it for 2 hours with a heavy object.

Cut in ½-inch slices and serve with a garnish of mashed potatoes.

> **NOTE**
> For more nutritious mashed potatoes, boil a pound of potatoes in their jackets for 30 minutes over medium heat. Remove, peel them and mash them while hot; add a Tbsp. of butter, an egg yolk, salt, pepper, nutmeg and half a cup of hot milk. Mix well and serve.

Italian immigrants — or rather, those from the regions we now call Italy — accepted the stews and started celebrating Sundays by cooking pasta. The arrival of this culinary context modified the eating habits of both natives and newcomers, combining the new contributions with the locally available ingredients. Thus Italian-Argentine cuisine was born, which identified ravioli and gnocchi with stewed beef and dishes of equivocal geography, such as *milanesa napolitana* and *raviolones sorrentinos* — invented not at the foot of Vesuvius but a couple of blocks from the Obelisk of Buenos Aires.

Although the first foundation of Buenos Aires failed due to a general famine, today visitors can find practically anything they want both in food and in entertainment. From the best tables of yesteryear comes the taste for beef tongue, potato pie (reminiscent of the Peruvian *causa*), and potato and egg *tortilla* (nothing like the Mexican bread) the best achievement of Spanish daily cooking. Colonial pies became delicious vegetable open-face pies.

Pizza and empanadas are the gastronomic crutch of the *porteño*, consumed without protocol in pizzerias and any time there is a need to eat at low cost and without culinary complications. The Argentine version of pizza had a plebeian origin. It was introduced by the Genoese around 1880 in the popular neighborhood of La Boca, where tango is said to have been born. The revolution of Argentine pizza did not take place until the second half of the 20th century, when it became a luxury food and was accepted by the upper middle class. Until that time it was a food for the poor, no more than a piece of dough smeared with tomato and anchovies. The Galician-Argentines reinvented Neapolitan pizza, adding garlic, fresh tomato, and mozzarella cheese (since called *muzarela*).

Even taking into account its *chinchulines* and *chimichurris,* Argentina is a country of international cooking. Foreigners are not subjected to concoctions of unknown origin, nor do they need wonder how to eat them or what seasonings lurk in them. The variety of dishes that Brazilians and Colombians sample at lunchtime every day, Argentines spread along the week. If they have eaten ravioli with sauce one day, they will want to try roast chicken on the following, and on the third day they will be begging for *milanesas.* The best cooks try their hand from time to time at an appetizing *arrollado de matambre* (stuffed rolled flank steak), which is baked in mud or patiently boiled and then served cold. Steaks, chicken, and milanesas are served with mashed vegetables (potatoes, pumpkin, sweet potatoes), French fries, or salads. Argentina is one of those countries in which it is always easy to get a salad with fresh vegetables and legumes. Pasta is kneaded the traditional way or bought in the very Argentine pasta factories, stores that offer a variety of ravioli, cannelloni, gnocchi, spaghetti, capelletti, agnolotti, and lasagna freshly made daily and ready to cook. Fish is abundant in seas, rivers, and lakes but not always found in the popular restaurants. At least once a year Argentines who vacation in Mar del Plata go to the port to get their fill of shellfish and other seafood.

Tourists tend to access the river at the Delta of the Paraná River (which can be easily accessed from Buenos Aires) or at Iguazú Falls, on the border with Brazil and Paraguay. In the river basin, the most popular fish are dorado, bream, pacú, and especially surubí, a large fish of the catfish family, a delicacy of the provinces that border the Paraná River and rarely found on the tables of Buenos Aires. Surubí is prepared fried, stewed, broiled, breaded, and in salads and soufflés. The ruins of the Jesuit Missions are the gateway to the Guarani cultural area, whose influence is felt in *chipá,* a type of manioc bread.

Talampaya,
La Rioja,
Argentina.

Locro (Argentina) #96

INGREDIENTS
(Makes 6 servings)
1 lb. flank steak
2 cups shelled white
  corn
1 onion

½ lb. pumpkin
¼ lb. bacon
¼ lb. pig skin
1 pig's leg
2 red sausages
1 Tbsp. paprika

1 tsp. ground cumin
4 quarts water
salt and pepper

SAUCE
2 green onions

1 Tbsp. beef fat
1 Tbsp. paprika
1 Tbsp. crushed red
  pepper

Soak the corn kernels in abundant water for 12 hours. Drain and boil in 4 quarts of water, together with the pig's leg and the skin, cut in thin strips, for an hour over medium heat.

Add the flank, cubed, the bacon, chopped, and the red sausages, sliced. Continue cooking, covered, for 45 minutes.

Add the onion, finely chopped, the pumpkin in one piece, the paprika and the cumin. Add salt and pepper and cook for 20 minutes.

Serve in individual bowls and cover with sauce.

SAUCE

Finely chop the green onions and sauté them in the beef fat for 10 minutes over medium heat. Season with paprika and crushed red pepper to taste.

> NOTE
> Besides the steak, bacon, and sausages, you can add ¼ lb. of large intestine cut in pieces and ½ lb. of tripe in strips.

The Northwest, historically linked to the culture and traffic of the Alto Peru, was receptive to the Inca influence of corn, potato, and quinoa. It is the country of votive meals and funeral banquets. The *mancafiesta* is one of the few occasions on which an Argentine will show an urge to eat in the streets among strangers. These popular fairs of the Puna bring back the traditional foods and drinks among people who are isolated most of the year. In the oases of the Calchaqui Valleys — an area of wild beauty — the best regional wines are produced, as well as the paprika that enhances the food of Salta.

Corn is king in humitas, tamales, and locros. Humita is prepared with ground kernels of fresh corn and goat or cow cheese. When it is served as a soup it is cooked in a pot; when it is cross-wrapped in corn husks, it is cooked in boiling water or among the embers. The tamale is a similar paste, prepared with corn flour and jerk beef or pork wrapped in corn husks and cooked in boiling water. Locro is an Andean stew made with boiled corn, ground and stewed with meats, cow intestine (*ocote*), sausage, and pumpkin. It may be garnished with a hot sauce.

More reserved for home-cooked meals are the hot, spicy tripe or chicken

Patagonian Lamb *(Argentina)* *#97*

INGREDIENTS
(Makes 6 servings)
1 4½-lb. leg of lamb, boned
2 carrots
2 leeks

1 red pepper
2 hardboiled eggs
3 Tbsp. butter

SAUCE
2 tomatoes

2 onions
2 Tbsp. butter
¼ lb. pitted black olives
¼ lb. pitted green olives
¼ cup port
salt and pepper

Photo: Carlos Mordo

Iguazu waterfalls,
Misiones,
Argentina.

PREPARATION

Chop the leeks, peel and grate the carrots and cut the pepper, without seeds or membranes, in thin strips. Sauté everything in 2 Tbsp. of butter for 10 minutes over medium heat. Set aside.

Sprinkle the leg of lamb with salt and pepper, wrap it in aluminum foil, greased with the remaining butter, and cook for an hour in the oven at high (425°F).

Take out of the oven, remove the aluminum foil and cut the lamb in ¾-inch slices. Heat the leek mixture. Place the lamb slices in a serving dish, cover them with the leeks and serve with the hot sauce. Decorate with the hardboiled eggs, sliced.

SAUCE

Cube the tomatoes, peeled and seeded, and finely chop the onions. Sauté them in 2 Tbsp. butter, together with the sliced black and green olives and the port, for 15 minutes over medium heat. Add salt and pepper and remove from heat. Heat at the time of serving.

stews, jerk stews (*sajta, charquisillo, chatasca*), *guaschalocro* (locro without meat or pumpkin), *frangollo* (a kind of cornmeal mush cooked with peppers and onions), and *mote* (corn softened in ash water, cooked and stewed with meat, intestines, and beans). Llama meat — which the Diaguita natives jerked to improve their locros — and quinoa soup have started a slow descent from the Puna to the avant-garde kitchens.

For dessert the offerings include walnuts with *cayote* sauce or cheeses (made of cow's or goat's milk) spread with cane honey, with prickly pear syrup, or with *cuaresmillo* jam (a small peach that ripens around Lent).

Filet Mignon (Argentina) #98

INGREDIENTS
(Makes 4 servings)
2 lbs. beef filet mignon
fine rock salt to taste

4 potatoes
cooking oil as needed
vegetables of the season

This deceptively simple dish requires a strict adherence to the steps to be followed.

Cut the meat in four steaks, loosely surrounding them with twine to keep their good shape. Heat a heavy iron griddle, slightly oiled, over high heat; once it is sizzling hot, place the steaks on it and allow the meat to seal, that is, to form a slight crust that will keep the juices inside. At that time, add half the salt you will use and lower the heat slightly to make sure the steaks will not burn. Once the juices start appearing on the surface of the meat, turn the steaks over, raising the heat to seal them on the other side; add the rest of the salt and cook for a few minutes. They must be juicy inside and crunchy outside.

Serve with fries and salad.

The old corn-based desserts, such as *anchi* and *mazamorra* (also called *api*), are usually made at home. Between Lima and Chile, Creole sweet-making remains in the form of empanadillas, *alfeñiques, gaznates,* and cane honey nougats. *Chicha*, mead, syrup, and *patay* (a bread made with cooked carob flour) are still made with the ripe pods of the carob — the high-protein bean prized by the ancient natives.

Mendoza and San Juan are the capitals of the arid but not unproductive area of Argentina. Darwin marveled at its irrigation cultivations and wrote, "The happy fortune of the people of Mendoza consists of wandering, eating and sleeping." The best Argentine wines are made in the oases of the pre-cordillera, especially Merlot, Malbec, Cabernet, and Syrah reds, but also whites and champagne.

Patagonia accepts several gastronomical readings: indigenous, Creole, immigrant, and tourist, not to mention the barbaric concoctions of the explorers of the 19th century. Natives and shipwrecked sailors ate seafood on the beach, deserted but striking with its natural reserves of birds and mammals. The fish restaurants are in Puerto Madryn, tourist capital of the Valdés Peninsula. While the motherland was being built in the trenches against the natives, the *revuelto Gramajo* was born as an emergency meal to appease all appetites with leftover ham, eggs, and French fries.

The Patagonian cuisine of the tour books was not created for low-class eateries. Lake trout and salmon are better suited to high-class tables. The marine creatures eaten in Ushuaia (Fuegian king crab, black hake) and the

Anchi *(Argentina) #99*

INGREDIENTS
(Makes 10 servings)
2¼ lb. corn flour
juice of 2 oranges

juice of 2 lemons
6 Tbsp. sugar
1 tsp. ground
    cinnamon

⅔ cup seedless white
    raisins
3 quarts water

PREPARATION

Heat the water in a thick-bottomed pot until it boils. Sprinkle the corn flour into the boiling water, stirring constantly with a wooden spoon; lower to minimum and simmer for 20 minutes until it starts to thicken.

Add the sugar, continue stirring and cooking for 5 minutes. Remove from heat, add the orange and lemon juices, strained, and the raisins. Stir well and pour into individual dessert dishes.

Cool in the fridge for an hour. Remove and sprinkle with cinnamon.

Serve very cold.

NOTE
The corn flour must be sprinkled into the water to prevent it from forming lumps.

wild game (deer and boar) raise the price of the typical menu. Sheep raised on the Magellanic and Fuegian estancias can be photographed in the shearing sheds and tasted on the spit, where they are called lamb. Between San Martín de los Andes, Bariloche, and Esquel lies the lake region, where smoked meats are prepared and ecotourism is promoted with organic vegetable gardens. The Negro River Valley is the Argentine equivalent of the Garden of the Hesperides, a producer of famed apples for export and of the southernmost wines of South America.

An Argentine breakfast will never boast steaming oatmeal or fried bacon.

Pastelitos *(Argentina)* #100

INGREDIENTS
(Makes 12)
2¼ lb. wheat flour
2 eggs

1 lb. lard
½ lb. quince loaf or sweet potato loaf
sugar as needed

water as needed
honey as needed
1 tsp. salt

PREPARATION

Place the flour on the table top; in a well in the center add half the lard, previously melted, and the salt. Mix well, add the eggs, beaten, and gradually add the amount of water needed to make a soft, smooth dough. Cover it with a cheesecloth and allow to rest for 40 minutes.

Roll the dough with a rolling pin to a thickness of ⅛ inch and cut it in 2½-inch squares.

To form the pastelitos, overlap 4 squares with their corners displaced so as to form an 8-point star. Place a portion of filling in the center and cover with another 4 squares distributed the same way as before.

Press around the filling to contain it and raise the corners of the dough slightly towards the center to shape them (see picture on page 182, top).

Heat the remaining lard well and fry the pastelitos for a few minutes until golden. Remove, sprinkle with sugar, pour a little honey over them and serve hot or at room temperature.

> NOTE
> The quince loaf or sweet potato loaf can be mashed first, adding a little honey to give it a smoother texture.

The ascetic cup of café au lait with buttered bread slices was promoted early on by the *Costumbrero de la Provincia Argentina de la Compañía de Jesús* (*The Book of Customs of the Argentine Province of the Company of Jesus*) for the first meal of the day. The native may improve it with biscuits, crescent rolls, and preserves. Many Argentines have *mate* for breakfast. In colonial times, mate was accompanied by *tortas fritas* (fritters) that Colombians would call arepas and Chileans sopaipillas.

As for desserts, gone are the days of street *mazamorras* — hawked by black lady vendors — and of rice pudding. The Spaniards introduced cow's

Cornstarch Alfajores with Dulce de Leche *(Argentina)* #101

INGREDIENTS
(Makes 12)
2 cups cornstarch
¾ cup wheat flour
¼ lb. butter
5 eggs

2 cups powdered sugar
2 Tbsp. grated coconut
1 tsp. vanilla extract
¼ cup sweet liqueur
1 tsp. baking powder

DULCE DE LECHE
4 quarts milk
2 lb. sugar

Beat 4 eggs for 5 minutes with a whisk and mix them with the powdered sugar, beating until creamy. Set aside.

Sift together the cornstarch, the flour and the baking powder. Pour out onto table top; in a well in the center, place the butter at room temperature, the vanilla extract, the liqueur and the egg and sugar cream. Work with your hands until firm.

Roll with a rolling pin to a thickness of 1¼ inch and cut in 1½-inch discs with a cookie cutter. Place the discs on a greased and floured cookie sheet.

Bake for 20 to 25 minutes at medium (350°F), until golden. Remove and cool.

To put together each alfajor, spread a ¼-inch coat of dulce de leche over one disc, cover with another, paint the edge with a little more dulce de leche and roll it on the grated coconut so that it sticks to the edge (see picture on page 182, bottom).

HOMEMADE DULCE DE LECHE
Heat 8 Tbsp. of sugar in a thick-bottomed pot for 20 minutes at medium, until it reaches caramel color. Add the milk and the remaining sugar and allow to reach boiling point.

Bring the heat to minimum, and simmer until it thickens, for about an hour.

HOMEMADE DULCE DE LECHE — EASY VERSION
Boil an unopened can of condensed milk for two hours in a saucepan filled with water. When you open it, its contents should have a rich caramel color.

---

milk which was caramelized to produce *dulce de leche*. This thick, brownish delicacy is a perfect companion for flan, last survivor of a lineage of Creole desserts that could not be obtained without a generous number of eggs and patient care by the stove. In the kitchens of Córdoba, Cuyo, and the vice royal Tucumán, the memory of sweet dishes such as *ambrosia, natilla,* and *leche asada* is still alive, but travelers must be persistent to find them. The least a traveler can be offered for dessert is slices of *queso y dulce* (cheese and jam loaf). They are so simple and unassuming that they say Borges craved them. We must not forget homemade pumpkin cubes in syrup or bread pudding dripping with caramel syrup. Sweets become a tourist attraction at Villa General Belgrano (pastries of Austro-Hungarian tradition), El Bolsón, and Bariloche (chocolates and confections made with fine fruits) and in the lower valley of the Chubut River (calorie-laden teas with Welsh cakes). Argentina is a large producer and exporter of natural honey. The most typical regional *alfajor* is that made in Santa Fe.

Photo: Roberto Cinti

Casa Pueblo,
Punta Ballena,
Uruguay.

*U*ruguay is a small, green country born in the heat of the struggle between the Brazilian Empire and the Argentine Confederation. Argentines delight in the quiet, winding streets of Colonia del Sacramento. On weekends they casually cross the River Plate, without setting their watches back or forth, knowing that in Uruguay the hours go by in a different fashion, that the beaches are clean, and that there is a parallel cuisine of beef and pasta, *mate* and *dulce de leche*. The gaucho lifestyle established the taste for barbecued beef, which both Argentines and Uruguayans consider the national treat.

All travelers mention Uruguayan barbecue. According to Concolorcorvo — an anonymous informer for the vice royal couriers — gauchos

Creole Beef Filets *(Uruguay)* #*102*

INGREDIENTS
(Makes 3 servings)
6 rump filets, cut thin
4 tomatoes

2 onions
1 red pepper
4 potatoes
½ cup oil

2 or 3 bay leaves
1 clove garlic
salt and pepper

PREPARATION

Finely slice the onions and the tomatoes, peeled and seeded, cut the pepper, without seeds or membranes, in thin strips, and mince the garlic. Set aside.

Peel the potatoes, slice them thinly and immerse them in a bowl of cold water to prevent discoloration.

Brown the filets in the oil for 5 minutes at high; remove half of them and set aside. Cover the remaining filets with half of the onion rings, half of the pepper strips and half of the tomato slices and the garlic. Drain the potato slices and add half of them on top of the tomatoes. Add salt and pepper; repeat the layers in the same order, starting with the rest of the filets, add some more salt and pepper and the bay leaves, cover and cook for 20 minutes, until the potatoes are tender.

> NOTE
> Should the cooking liquid evaporate, you may add beef broth as needed.

(*gauderios*) practiced a lazy lifestyle of easy eating. The country is so prodigal, he says, that "it freely offers the idle bread, meat, and fish in abundance." In his chronicle he points out that when hunger struck in the midst of a journey, the gauderio might kill a young bull or cow just to barbecue its flank, or any other cut of his preference, leaving the rest behind." According to Hermann Burmeister (1856), those traveling along the Banda Oriental pay for all their food, except the meat.

Half the population of Uruguay, it seems, has lunch and dinner in Montevideo. At the Mercado del Puerto (Harbor Market) food stalls mix with meat grills and seafood restaurants, very crowded on Saturdays at noon.

Chajá *(Uruguay)* #103

INGREDIENTS
(Makes 6 servings)
Sponge cake
1½ cups flour
½ cup sugar
6 eggs
1 tsp. vanilla extract

1 Tbsp. butter (for the mold)
1 Tbsp. flour (for the mold)

MERINGUE
1 cup. sugar

6 egg whites
1 tsp. cream of tartar
1 Tbsp. butter (for the mold)
1 Tbsp. flour (for the mold)

FILLING
1 cup whipping cream
7 oz. dulce de leche (see Recipe #101)
4 strawberries
2 canned peaches

SPONGE CAKE

Beat the sugar with the eggs and the vanilla extract for 15 minutes with the electric mixer. Gradually add the sifted flour, blending in gently until smooth.

Pour the batter in a rectangular 12 x 16-inch cake pan, buttered and floured.

Preheat the oven to medium (350°F) and bake for 30 minutes until golden. Remove and set aside.

MERINGUE

Beat the egg whites until they form stiff peaks; add the sugar in a fine shower, add the cream of tartar and mix gently with folding movements.

Grease and flour an oven sheet, place the meringue in a decorator bag with a wide tip and form six circles, about 1½ to 2 inches in diameter and 1¼ inch thick. Preheat the oven to low (285°F) and bake for 40 minutes, until the meringue is completely dry. Remove and set aside.

FILLING

Beat the whipping cream with a hand beater for about 10 minutes, until the cream forms peaks as you lift it. Chill in the fridge for an hour.

Dice the canned peaches and slice the strawberries thin. Set aside.

MAKING THE CHAJA

Cut 12 discs from the sponge cake with a round cutter the size of the meringue circles.

Using one sponge cake disc as the base, sprinkle it with the syrup from the canned peaches and spread a coat of milk jam over that. Cover it with a meringue disc, spread another coat of milk jam and cover with another sponge cake disc.

Cover the top disc with whipped cream, spread the diced peaches over the cream and decorate with the strawberry slices.

NOTE
Chaja can also be covered all over with whipped cream, sprinkling pieces of broken-up meringue on it.

Chivito al Plato (Uruguay) #104

INGREDIENTS
(Makes 4 servings)
4 beef sirloin filets, cut thin
4 thin slices baked ham
4 thin strips smoked bacon

4 slices mozzarella cheese
4 slices white bread
4 leaves lettuce
2 chopped hardboiled eggs
1 Tbsp. chopped green

olives
2 Tbsp. sliced mushrooms

PREPARATION

Preheat an iron grid and cook the filets for 5 minutes on each side at high; place the ham, mozzarella, and smoked bacon on each of them and continue cooking for 5 minutes, until the cheese melts.

Remove; place a slice of bread on each plate, cover with a lettuce leaf, place the steak on top of the lettuce and cover it with hardboiled egg, olives and the mushrooms sautéed in butter.

> **NOTE**
> To prevent the meat from sticking to the grid at the beginning of the cooking time, brush the surface of the grid with vegetable oil.

The famous street market of Tristán Narvaja started out as a food market that later extended to accommodate booksellers, antiquarians, automotive spare parts dealers, plant vendors, and many others to become one of the main attractions of the capital.

Uruguay's interior is a land of gauchos, *estancias* (ranches), and small cities where flavorful country cooking is abundant and the ancient customs of siesta and street *mate* are still practiced. Every village has its wooded park and its rivers with clean, shaded banks, where it is common to find small restaurants offering a beef *chivito* — the national sandwich — and a beer.

On the coast of Rocha, where the thriving Vaquería del Mar ("country of wild cows") flourished at the end of the 17th century, there are gaucho fishermen who prepare dogfish fillets and seaweed fritters. The palm groves of Rocha, threatened by the expansion of cattle raising, constitute a notable natural reserve. The *butiaseros* make rum and liqueur from the fruit of the butiá palm and sell it along the road.

Salvo Palace,
Montevideo,
Uruguay.

Photo: Fausto Giaccone-Ag. Anzenberger

Natives in a colony in the Paraguayan Chaco.

*P*araguay appeared on the route the Spanish took in search of the silver of Peru. When Ulrico Schmidel, a participant in the first Spanish expeditions to the River Plate (16th century), sailed up the Paraguay River looking for amazons and chieftains smeared with gold, he discovered more mundane details: the natives were well provided with grains and root vegetables, game, and fish. In that tropical isolation, where bureaucratic and religious precepts could be interpreted without inconvenient mediators, there flourished an unusual mixing of Spanish and native. Far from the sea and the ports, the Creole slept well-fed and in good company — no small achievement in a recently conquered South America.

Chipá (Paraguay) #105

INGREDIENTS
(Makes 24)
11 oz. manioc starch
11 oz. grated soft cheese

¾ cup wheat flour
¼ cup whipping cream
2 egg yolks
salt

PREPARATION

Sift the manioc starch with the flour and a pinch of salt. Pour on the table top forming a crown and pour the egg yolks, lightly beaten, and the soft cheese in the center.

Knead well for 10 minutes, gradually adding the cream until smooth. Cover with a cheesecloth and allow to rest for 20 minutes on the table top.

Take small portions of the dough, form walnut-sized balls and place them on a greased cookie sheet.

Preheat the oven to medium (350ºF) and bake for 15 minutes until golden.

NOTE
The cream may be replaced by the same amount of milk.
It is important not to exceed the baking time; otherwise the chipas will take on a bitter taste.

Today as in yesteryear, Paraguayan cooking is based on inexpensive products, easily obtainable both in urban vegetable gardens and in rural cultivations. One has to be very poor not to have a ration of manioc starch, honey, cheese freshly made with cow's milk, fruit and vegetables from the garden, lard or oil, and a fire for cooking. The main dishes are prepared with manioc (*mandió*), a root vegetable as highly prized as the potato in the Andean countries or bread in the River Plate area.

In Paraguay, the term *sopa* (soup) is reserved for the national dish: *sopa paraguaya*. This baked pie has no need of spoons; it is, rather, a soufflé and must be high and airy. Sopa is a home meal, unlike *chipá*, the daily bread in the Guarani provinces, which is more street-oriented. It is prepared on Sundays to share with relatives, for Christmas, birthdays, and weddings. What is called soup in other places is called broth here. The liquid soup is

Chipá Guazú (Paraguay) #106

INGREDIENTS
(Makes 6 servings)
6 ears of corn
3 eggs, separated
3 onions
3 tsp. sugar
6 oz. lard
6 oz. paraguay cheese
9 oz. cheese curds
banana leaves as needed
1 Tbsp. lard (for the mold)
salt

PREPARATION

Grate thecorn kernels and set aside.

Finely chop the onions and sauté them in the lard for 10 minutes over medium heat. Add the sugar, the salt, the grated corn kernels, the cheese in small pieces and the curds; mix well and set aside.

Separate the yolks from the whites and beat the whites until they form stiff peaks.

Add the yolks, one at a time, mixing gently after each addition to blend them well, and add to the previous mixture.

Grease an oven pan, cover the base with banana leaves and pour the mixture evenly into it.

Preheat the oven to medium (350ºF) and bake for 35 minutes, until golden.

Remove, allow to cool slightly and serve warm.

> **NOTE**
> The banana leaves prevent the mixture from sticking to the oven pan. You may do without them by greasing and flouring the pan.

Caburé Aramiró (Paraguay) #107

INGREDIENTS
(Makes 6 servings)
18 oz. cornstarch
3 Tbsp. lard
3 eggs
5 Tbsp. salt water
11 oz. grated paraguay cheese
1 tsp. anise seeds

PREPARATION

Pour the cornstarch on the table top forming a crown; add the lard, previously melted, the grated cheese, the eggs and the anise seeds in the center. Add the salt water and knead well until smooth.

Distribute the dough uniformly on a 1¼-inch wooden cylinder and cook over red-hot coals for approximately 15 minutes, turning the cylinder continuously so that it cooks evenly.

> **NOTE**
> The caburé will be ready to eat when the surface of the dough is puffy.
> To make salt water dissolve a Tbsp. of rock salt in a quart of lukewarm water.

So'o Yosopy *(Paraguay)* #*108*

INGREDIENTS
(Makes 8 servings)
3½ lb. beef chuck
1 onion
1 green pepper

2 cloves garlic
1 tsp. oregano
1 Tbsp. chopped parsley
2 quarts water
3 Tbsp. lard

salt
3 Tbsp. very thin noodle
   strands
1 cup rice
2 cups water

PREPARATION

Grind the beef in a mortar to break it into pieces and make it release its juices; place in a bowl, add two quarts of water, stir and set aside.

Finely chop the onion, the green pepper, without seeds or membranes, and the cloves of garlic, and sauté them in the lard for 10 minutes over medium heat. Add the beef and the water, mix and cook for 15 minutes, until it breaks into a boil. Add salt, remove from heat and add the oregano and the parsley.

Cook the rice in half a quart of water for 15 minutes and the noodles, cook for another 5 minutes and add to the concoction.

Serve hot in individual bowls.

> NOTE
> Do not overheat this dish so that the rice will not be overcooked.

the *borí-borí,* a kind of *ajiaco* (a stew made with vegetables and meat), although far from the grandeur of its Colombian relative.

The Guarani fast food is also manioc-based: cut up in small pieces and mixed with ground beef (*mandió-reviro*) or mashed with raw beef and garlic leaves (*payagüá-mascada*). On the edges of the Guarani rivers stands the empire of the *mbeyú,* whose geographic spread can be attested by the Brazilian *beijus.* After losing the coconut milk of Bahia and the chestnuts of Pará, this indigenous concoction of deep folk tradition reaches the Paraguayan table as a simple omelet made of manioc starch, Paraguayan cheese, and cow's milk.

Paraguay attracted the first cattle drives of the Cono Sur. Goats and sheep arrived from the Alto Perú. It is accepted as fact that the seven

Sopa Paraguaya (Paraguay) #109

INGREDIENTS
(Makes 6 servings)
18 oz. corn flour
3 onions
½ lb. lard
½ lb. paraguay cheese (soft cheese)
½ lb. curds

6 egg whites
6 egg yolks
2 Tbsp. oil (for the pan)
banana leaves as needed
salt

Cut the onions in thin strips and mix them with the lukewarm melted lard. Add the corn flour, mix all ingredients well and allow to rest for an hour.

Beat the egg whites until they form stiff peaks. Set aside.

Add the soft cheese in small pieces, the curds, the salt, the yolks, beaten, and finally the whites. Mix well and set aside.

Grease an oven pan with oil, cover the base with banana leaves and pour the mixture evenly into it.

Preheat the oven to high (425°F) and bake for 45 minutes, until golden.

Serve hot.

> **NOTE**
> The sopa paraguaya is done when a knife inserted in its center comes out clean. The banana leaves may be left out by using a non-stick pan.

---

bulls and the cow mentioned in the chronicle of Ruy Díaz de Guzmán originally came from Brazil, inaugurating border smuggling, as Paraguayan as *mate* and oranges. Animals and drivers would leave their mark on the gaucho lifestyle, later symbolized by the estancia and barbecues made on grills and spits, typical of the River Plate basin and the south of Brazil.

The Jesuits, in turn, negotiated with the Guaranis, making them monogamous in exchange for huge meat rations. The Jesuit Missions — whose ruins can be visited starting at Encarnación — gave rise to an agricultural export business with national labor, its own language (Guaran), and regional production, based mainly on the cultivation of mate tea (*Hylex paraguaiensis*).

Uruguayans and Paraguayans consider mate a national custom. In Paraguay it is drunk hot (in a gourd, sipped through a straw) or prepared with cold water, the refreshing *tereré,* almost always accompanied by digestive herbs that are sold at the market. No productive nor idle day can be thought of without tereré, just as there is no siesta without a hammock. Uruguay does not produce mate tea but it is the most *matero* country of South America. Mate is consumed in the Rio Grande fashion, in a large gourd and *sin palo* (in powdered form).

Traditionally, all through the Cono Sur, whether hosts were rich or poor,

Photo: Ron Lovelace

Sea lions, Cabo Blanco, Santa Cruz, Argentina.

the first show of hospitality was mate. No one goes into a *rancho* (hut) without being offered a mate right away, affirms German traveler Erwin von Hase in his *Bosquejos argentinos* (*Argentine Sketches*). In order to *matear* (drink mate) you need a gourd or small container, similar to those sold to tourists as souvenirs; mate tea (a product commercially packaged and sold at grocery stores); a *bombilla* (drinking straw); a *caldera* (a kind of kettle invented to pour water into the mate, similar to the Argentine *pava*); pure water kept very hot without reaching boiling point; and a thermos bottle to keep more water at the right temperature, without which the mate cannot roam about. Any place and time is right to drink mate. It is shared among friends and neighbors, at work or during leisure moments.

In Argentina there are regional, urban, and rural mates. The small gourd is preferred, as is the mate tea with *palo* (stem), less powdered; it is drunk bitter or sweetened with sugar. The Chilean mate is restricted mostly to rural areas. In Brazil, from Mato Grosso to the border with Uruguay, mate is drunk cold (*tereré*) or hot (*chimarrão*).

While at mealtime Argentina looks toward the pampas and Chile toward the Pacific, the highly praised Andean sun brings them together in a common taste for wine, which they produce mainly in the Valley of the Maipo

(Chile) and in the oases of Mendoza and San Juan (Argentina), regions that have become a symbol of quality in the most important wine markets of the world. The first vineyards ripened in the Captainship of Chile and were exported to colonial Tucumán to grace the tables of the convents of the first Argentine city (Santiago del Estero). The wineries — called *viñas* in Chile — were given the names of pioneer families who started the modern industry in the 19th century, importing French stock. In many cases, travelers can visit their ancestral homes and taste their wines. The wine culture has also taken root in southern Brazil and in Uruguay. Uruguayan wines, produced mainly in the region of Carmelo and Canelones, have reached high quality. While in Argentina and Chile red wines are favorites to accompany meats and white wines are drunk with fish and seafood, in Uruguay the preferred wines are rosé and claret.

Whether due to laziness or pragmatism, and in order to satisfy their hunger right away and at low cost, the inhabitants of this end of the world — often forced to eat on the go — venerate the handy slices of beef and various cold meats between two slices of bread; if at all possible, they like those combined with vegetables and even with fried eggs. Most famous among the refreshing national sandwiches are the Chilean *Barros Luco* and *Barros Jarpa,* the Argentine *pebete* and *choripán,* and the patriotic Uruguayan *chivito.*

Recipe Glossary *(Cono Sur)*

ARGENTINA

CHALA: husk.
Choclo: corn.
LARD: may be replaced by corn or olive oil.
LOCRO: thick stew of cracked corn, meats, pumpking, potatoes, etc.
MATAMBRE: butterflied flank steak.

MONDONGO: tripe.
PASTELITOS: small pastry.

CHILE

MERQUÉN: ground pepper used by the Mapuches. May be replaced by regular crushed red pepper.

PARAGUAY

ANDAÍ: squash.
LOCOTE: red, yellow or green hot pepper.
PARAGUAY CHEESE: semi-hard yellow cheese.

BRAZIL

Sugarloaf Mountain, Rio de Janeiro, Brazil. Photo: Panoramic Images

Stalls selling dried meats, pork, mutton, venison, pacas and porcupines, various game. Sacks of the white manioc flour, golden plantains, yellow squashes, green beans, native fruit, oranges. On tin plates in slave quarters they served sarapatel, bean stew, fish casseroles. Some country folk ate with their glass of rum beside them...

—Jorge Amado, *Gabriela, Cloves and Cinnamon*

The fusion of peoples and cultures is the most characteristic aspect of Brazilian civilization. This mix is also the rule in its national cuisine. Brazilian dishes combine liquids with solids, hot with cold, salt with sweet, meat and fish with vegetables and legumes, flour with fruit. One eats a mix of everything that is on the table, combining the flavors according to the taste of the diner.

In the 16th century, when globalization hit the world's spice and food trades, the Portuguese brought to Brazil produce and plants from the Orient. The humble daily food of the native and the African diversified into tastier dishes adapted to the modern palate. The Portuguese incorporated spices in to their dishes during their preparation, rather than season them after cooking or roasting as the natives did.

Wheat bread, today's normal breakfast (*café do manhá*), was expensive and hard to find in colonial markets. Brazilians were accustomed to cornmeal (*farinha de milho*), which is preferred by the people of Sao Paulo, but above all to manioc, which has no substitute in the Northeast. Manioc is one of the fundamental pillars of Brazilian cooking. Manioc flour (*farinha*) is used in nearly every meal, from the *gaúchos churrasco* (steak) to Amazonian fish, even fruit: mango with farinha, *açai* (the fruit of an Amazonian palm) with farinha, oranges with farinha.

When the *bandeirante's* expeditions that ventured into the unconquered and unknown interior ran out of manioc, part of the expedition was left behind to grow it and prepare the farinha. Enormous *Terra Brasilis* was conquered on foot on rations of manioc. Natives, blacks, whites, and those of mixed blood all depend on this basic food of tropical kitchens. It is called *macaxeira* in the northeast, *mandioca* in Sao Paulo, *aipim* in Rio de Janeiro. Mixed with meat or other ingredients it is known as *farofa,* which is almost a food in itself. The use of manioc flour preceded rice by a couple of centuries, the latter being introduced from Asia to reinforce the ordinary person's diet, which consists of manioc farinha, rice, dried meat,

Photo: Fausto Giaccone-Ag. Anzenberger

Marajo Island,
Brazil.

beans (*feijoes*), corn and *rapadura* (tablets of brown sugar). All classes accompany their meals with rice, which is also the main course with chicken, certain herbs, and fruit that have given it regional fame, such *piquí* (or *pequi*), an aromatic fruit very much appreciated by people from Goias.

Since there is not one Brazilian cuisine but several, it is impossible to choose a single national dish. If one had to settle for only one, many would opt for the complete *feijoada*. The ingredients of today's feijoada differ little from the basic diet that fed the slaves on a well-provided estate. From Portugal they got the secrets of boiled meat and vegetables (*cozido*) and feijoada entered the treat category. Black beans are cooked with pieces of pork or beef; up to a dozen different bits are used, from jerked meat to bacon, sausage, ox tail, pig's ear, and trotters. It is brought to table with an accompaniment of rice, manioc flour, or *farofa* (toasted manioc flour with ground meat), a mild vinaigrette, *couve* (a Brazilian vegetable originally

Shrimp Soup *(Brazil)* #*110*

INGREDIENTS
(Makes 6 servings)
1½ lb. clean, fresh
   shrimp
2 sweet potatoes

2 egg yolks
2 tsp. cornstarch
2 Tbsp. chopped
   parsley
1 clove garlic

1 Tbsp. butter
1 Tbsp. corn oil
1 Tbsp. tomato paste
1 Tbsp. cream cheese
1 cup whipping cream

2 cups water
juice of one lemon
salt and pepper

PREPARATION

Sprinkle the shrimp with the lemon juice, add salt and pepper, the chopped garlic and parsley, and sauté in the oil and butter together with the tomato paste for 5 minutes. Set aside.

Peel the sweet potatoes, cut them in small pieces and boil them in 2 cups of water over medium heat for 15 minutes. Take them out and reserve the water.

Put the sweet potatoes through the blender with 4 Tbsp. of the water and mix them with the egg yolks, slightly beaten; add the cornstarch, previously dissolved in a little water, the whipping cream, and the cream cheese. Lightly soften the mixture by adding 3 Tbsp. of the water in which the sweet potatoes were boiled.

Add the shrimp together with another 4 Tbsp. of the same water, mix well and simmer for 5 minutes to finish cooking and allow the soup to thicken.

> TIP
> The cornstarch must be dissolved in a little cold water before blending in with the rest of the ingredients.

from Portugal), and slices of orange. When Brazilians wish to convey their opinion that the treat is one of the best, they call it *feijoada carioca,* even if they are not from Rio de Janeiro.

Brazilians get involved in the kitchen with visceral dedication. Cuisine is the second or third religion of the country. Its shrine is the market, where the visitor can admire the enormous variety of meats, fruits, legumes, vegetables, sauces (*molhos*), and condiments (*temperos*). In villages and by the roadside one finds *caipira* cooking (country cooking), tasty and fresh. Many cities such as Belém, Salvador, and Olinda are known for their traditional menus that are eaten out of doors. The social importance of foods explains the primary place food has as offerings to the *orixás,* deities of Afro-Catholic syncretism.

Farofa de Dendê *(Brazil)* #*111*

INGREDIENTS
(Makes 4 servings)
1 small onion, finely chopped
2 Tbsp. dendê oil
salt
1 Tbsp. toasted manioc flour
1 Tbsp. clean, fresh shrimp

PREPARATION

Fry the chopped onion in half the oil, over medium heat, for 10 minutes. Add salt and gradually add the manioc flour, stirring constantly with a wooden spoon to prevent it from lumping. Set aside.

Fry the shrimp in the rest of the oil for 2 minutes, adding them to the mixture above.

Serve as a side dish.

NOTE
Once cooked, the manioc flour should be dry and loose.

Photo: Richard Bickel–Black Star

Salvador of Bahia, Brazil.

Crab Casquinhas (Brazil) #112

INGREDIENTS
(Makes 6 servings)
2¼ lb. crab meat
2 tomatoes
2 cloves garlic
2 onions

2 lemons
2 cheiro peppers
2 slices white bread
2 Tbsp. prepared coffee
2 Tbsp. vinegar
2 Tbsp. olive oil

4 Tbsp. coconut milk
2 Tbsp. grated cheese
2 Tbsp. bread crumbs
3 egg yolks
1 tsp. cornstarch
1 Tbsp. Cachaça or

some other high
proof rum
1 bay leaf
1 bunch coriander
1 qt. water
salt

Prepare some broth with the water, chopped coriander, a tomato, seeded and quartered, the lemon rinds and the cheiro peppers, seeded, without membranes and cut in halves, letting it boil for 30 minutes. Add salt and the crab meat and continue boiling until it turns reddish, approximately 15 minutes. Cool, drain the meat and discard the broth.

Cube the bread, dip it in the coffee and mix it with the vinegar, oil, coconut milk, the crushed garlic, the onions, finely chopped, the remaining tomato, seeded and diced, and the bay leaf. Cook for 15 minutes, covered, over low heat; turn heat to minimum and add the lemon juice, the cornstarch, previously dissolved in cold water, and two egg yolks, beaten, stirring as you do. Turn off immediately, add the cheese, the bread crumbs, the remaining egg yolk, beaten, the cachaça and the crab meat. Pour the mixture into a casserole dish and complete cooking in hot oven for 10 minutes.

Serve hot in the crab shells.

From domestic zeal in colonial kitchens came the habit of giving special attention to the choosing of ingredients and seasonings, and in taking meticulous care over the preparation of meals. In other words, Brazilian cooking did not evolve to satisfy impatient diners. Judging from his writings, Charles Darwin was one such: "When thoroughly exhausted by fatigue and hunger we timorously hinted that we should be glad of our meal, the pompous and, (though true) most unsatisfactory answer was 'It will be ready when it is ready.'"

Certain dishes, such as *azul-marinho* (a fish and plantain hot-pot) from the coast of Sao Paulo, Paraná's *barreado* (meat stew), and tasty *paneladas* (dishes cooked in earthenware pots), take time to prepare and some chickens are in the pot for three days before going to table. In *tacacá* (a shrimp soup) and *maniçoba* (prepared with manioc leaves and meats), both dishes from Paraná, the native formula for preparing the poisonous manioc also requires several days of preparation.

European travelers of the 19th century spoke highly of the qualities of Brazilian tables. Sir Richard Francis Burton went so far as to claim that Brazilian hospitality was what most delayed travel in that country. According to Johann Moritz Rugendas — archetype of that century's world travelers — even strangers are accorded a warm reception.

Xinxim Hen *(Brazil)* #*113*

INGREDIENTS
(Makes 4 servings)
1 4½ lb. hen
¼ lb. dry shrimp
1 small onion
2 cloves garlic

4 Tbsp. chopped coriander
1 red pepper
½ cup cashews
1 bay leaf
1 tsp. peeled, roasted
   peanuts

1 tsp. grated ginger root
1 Tbsp. dendê oil
chicken broth as needed
juice of one lemon
salt and pepper

PREPARATION

Finely chop the onion and the pepper, without membranes or seeds, and crush the garlic. Fry all the above in oil for 10 minutes in a thick-bottomed pan. Add the bay leaf, coriander, salt and pepper and put in the hen, cut in 8 pieces. Cook for about 30 minutes, covered, over low heat.

Peel the shrimp and process them with the cashews, the roasted peanuts and the ginger. Put them in the mixture, add the lemon juice and gradually add the hot broth as needed. Continue cooking for 30 minutes over low heat until the meat is tender.

Serve in individual bowls.

Unexpected guests are offered little pies, *cocada* (nougat made with grated coconut and molasses), a glass of *coalhada* (curds or homemade yoghurt), *cafezinho* (a demitasse of coffee), or some refreshing drink. Abundance without waste is the measure of ever-renewed hospitality.

Brazilians take breakfast and lunch early. Supper is, as in monasteries, eaten before sundown. From Monday to Sunday the ideal dish consists of rice and beans (*feijao*) — always hot, never cold — accompanied by three *misturas* that vary from day to day and are served on a separate plate: meat (beef, pork, or chicken), salads (fresh and green), and *rehogado* (vegetables cooked in the oven or in a casserole). Rice is nearly always cooked just once during the day, enough to cover both meals. The base of feijao should be prepared to last for three days. If these two main pillars of Brazilian

Vatapá *(Brazil)* #114

INGREDIENTS
(Makes 6 servings)
1¼ lb. fresh codfish
1 qt. water
2 onions (1 for the
  broth)
3 tomatoes (1 for the
broth)
2 cloves garlic (1 for the
  broth)
2 bunches coriander (1
  for the broth)
1 cup shelled, roasted
  peanuts
½ lb. dry shrimp
½ cup cashews
3 tsp. grated ginger root
¼ cup corn flour
salt
1 coconut
6 Tbsp. dendê oil

PREPARATION

Cut the codfish in medium-sized pieces and place in a quart of water with a Tbsp.
salt, together with one onion, finely chopped, one diced tomato, peeled and seeded,
one crushed clove of garlic and one bunch of coriander, chopped; boil for 25
minutes over medium heat. Take out the fish, remove the bones and cartilage.
Strain the broth, discard the vegetables and reserve the liquid.

Grate the remaining onion and cube the tomatoes, peeled and seeded; add them to
the broth and put in the crushed garlic, the chopped peanuts, the rest of the
coriander, chopped, the shrimp, the cashews, the ginger and the corn flour. Correct
the amount of salt and cook over medium heat (350º F) for 15 minutes, stirring
slowly. Set aside.

Grate the coconut, squeeze the pulp with your hands to obtain the resulting milk
and add both to the mixture, together with 2 Tbsp. dendê oil and the codfish.
Continue cooking over low heat for 15 minutes.

Put 2 Tbsp. dendê oil in the bottom of a deep rectangular pan. Pour the mixture
into it, pressing it firmly to make it easier to unmold, and cover with the remaining
dendê oil. Heat for 5 minutes in hot oven (425º F), unmold and serve hot with
white rice.

TIP
It is important for
the mixture to be the
right thickness when
pressed into the
mold so that it will
keep its shape when
unmolded.

cuisine are always equally good, it is in the misturas that chefs can excel, either offering a delicious *bife acebolado* (steak and onions), a tasty fried sausage (*lingüiça*), pork ribs, chicken joints à la casserole, or fried fish.

Cool drinks such as lemonade or fruit juices are drunk, and the meal winds up with dessert (*sobremesa*). In smart or more popular restaurants, this ideal menu comes under the name of *refeiçao,* presented on various plates simultaneously and nearly always with beer to drink. The national fizzy drink is *guaraná* with the flavor of an Amazon fruit.

For eaters who are in a hurry, like Darwin, food comes by the kilo or as a ready meal (*prato feito*), an economical fast dish that brings rice, feijao, a piece of meat, salad, a fried egg, and manioc flour, all on the same plate. In some Sao Paulo restaurants certain dishes are served on assigned days of the week: today *virado* (beans à la paulista), tomorrow *dobradinha* (tripe). Wednesdays and Saturdays are usually reserved for feijoada with its best ingredients. Pasta, which can be as much part of a Sunday meal as the feijoada, is never a main dish as is the case in Argentina. It is incorporated into the symphony of flavors on the Brazilian table. The main meal is served at midday (in a restaurant it is no use asking for feijoada for supper). At night the misturas change but rice and feijao still dominate the meal.

In Brazil, "bar" means a place to drink. The most popular version is the *boteco* or *botequim. Lanchonetes* are sandwich bars and very much cater to passers-by. They are usually well stocked with *pastéis* (pasties or turnovers), *salgadinhos* (chicken, shrimp, or cheese croquettes) and *pao de queijo* (cheese and cornmeal brioche), something like Columbian *pandebono* (manioc bread). Some lanchonetes are a paradise for fruit juices (*sucos*) and milkshakes (*vitaminas)* — the avocado variety (*abacate*) should not be missed. This fruit is cultivated throughout Latin America but in Brazil it is valued as a drink and as a dessert (with sugar and milk).

Rio de Janeiro was the great imperial capital of Brazil. On November 11, 1889, the emperor Dom Pedro II and a great number of courtiers — more than three thousand were invited — attended a bizarre banquet on the Ilha Fiscal, an event which passed into Brazilian history as the swansong of the monarchy, since four days later the Republic was instated. Coffee, which in many restaurants and hotels is "on the house," was a symbol of imperial economics (1822 to 1889) and was witness to a period of great change in Brazilian history, when the era of mule transport

Photo: Ricardo Malta-Black Star

Women from
Bahia in Salvador,
Brazil.

gave way to the railroad and slavery to immigration. The best lands for growing coffee were in Sao Paulo and Minas Gerais, where workers from crumbling northeastern sugar plantations and gold and diamond mines found employment. Ouro Preto, the most attractive colonial city in Brazil (and probably in South America), owes its fame to gold and its name to coffee (*ouro*: gold, *preto*: black).

The main culinary traditions in Brazil come from the Northeastern and Amazonian regions and from mining. In the Amazon they are based on hunting and fishing. Tourists visiting Manaos take excursions into the jungle and eat *macaco moqueado* (monkey barbecue) like jungle peoples. Fish is grilled over hot coals, smoked, stewed, made into *bolinhos* (croquettes), with fried banana and *farinha* seasoned with local herbs or stock of wild manioc. Some are so big that they come to the table under names normally associated with beef: roast tenderloin of pirarucú, tambaquí cutlets. Stock made with piranha heads is considered an aphrodisiac. Fruit is exquisite, abundant, and cheap. Good manners among the native people require that visitors on arrival be offered a hammock full of fruit in the shade.

Feijoada *(Brazil)* #*115*

INGREDIENTS
(Makes 8 servings)
2¼ lb. black beans
1 pig's tail
1 pig's ear
1 pig's leg
¾ lb. pork loin
¾ lb. pork breast

¾ lb. jerk beef
¼ lb. sausage
¼ lb. pepperoni
½ lb. pork tongue
½ lb. beef tongue
¼ lb. beef ribs
¼ lb. smoked bacon
2 bay leaves

2 onions
2 cloves garlic
2 Tbsp. olive oil
3 qt. water
salt

MANIOC FAROFA
1¼ lb. manioc flour

1 onion
1 clove garlic
1 Tbsp. butter
1 Tbsp. seedless black
    raisins
salt

PREPARATION

Soak the beans in water for 12 hours.

Wash the jerk beef, the pork loin, the beef and pork tongues and the pig's tail, ear and foot thoroughly and separately until they are clean. Cover them with water and let them rest in the fridge for 6 hours.

Put the beans in water, together with the bay leaf and the bacon, cut up in pieces, and cook for an hour over medium heat.

Add salt, put in the beef and pork tongues, skinned and cut up in large chunks, the pork loin and breast, whole, the ribs, the jerk beef, and the pig's tail, ear and foot. Continue cooking for another hour, covered, over medium heat, constantly skimming the fat off the surface of the broth. Add hot water as needed so that the meats are covered at all times.

Sauté the garlic, previously crushed, in the olive oil and add to the pot with the onions, quartered, the sausage and the pepperoni, both whole. Continue cooking for 30 minutes over medium heat.

Strain out two ladlefuls of beans, mash them with a fork until they form a paste, and add them to the pot to thicken the mixture. Lower the heat to minimum and simmer another 10 to 15 minutes.

Serve with manioc farofa.

MANIOC FAROFA

Finely chop the onion and fry it in butter for 10 minutes, together with the crushed garlic; finely sprinkle the manioc flour into it stirring constantly, and continue cooking over medium heat for 15 minutes, until the flour starts browning. Remove from heat, add salt and raisins, cover and allow to cool.

> **NOTE**
> Feijoada can also be served with white rice and orange wedges.

The traditional cuisine of Pará is perhaps the most unchanged and least known of Brazilian cooking. In Belém every visit should start in the Ver-o-Peso market. This gigantic food emporium in Amazonia's hinterland will confirm at a glance the complex variety of regional ingredients. Once among the huge and colorful agglomeration of motley stalls, buyers can eat vatapá fish mold, tacacá soup, *maniçoba* (manioc leaves and meat), açaí palm fruit, and many other traditional indigenous dishes that, for lack of the necessary ingredients, are not found outside the region. This whole neighborhood of frying pans and cooking pots must be home to the greatest concentration of bits and pieces of food, aromas, and calories in the world. The tourist can wander though warehouses packed to the roof with fruit, vegetables, and fish. Here one can purchase jars of *tucupí,* a sauce based on the juice of poisonous manioc used in the preparation of wild duck. Mixed with manioc starch and enriched with jambu leaves and shrimp it makes *tacacá,* a substantial soup. Street vendors prepare it by the road but it is a task reserved for women. In bygone days it was the work of the tacacazeira mulatto women. Traditionally it is served in small, black earthenware bowls.

In the northeast there are coastal and inland cuisines. The characteristic ingredient is *carne de sol,* a sun-dried meat like Andean jerked beef. It is the coarsest meat in Brazil but in this region it is preferred to fresh meat. On the coast *peixada* and *moquecas,* seafood stews, soups, and stock, are favorites. The first consists of pieces of fish broiled in pots with vegetable seasoning, hard-boiled eggs, and coriander (*coentro*). The final touch is coconut milk, and it is accompanied with white rice.

Fish farming, which prospers in the small catchment dams (*açudes*) scattered throughout the countryside of the Northeast, extends the consumption of fish to the interior where traditionally tripe and meat meals such as the native *paçoca* are offered. This is made with roast meat and

Preparation of wild casava flour, San Raimundo, Brazil.

Photo: Fausto Giaccone-Ag. Anzenberger

Cuscuz Paulista (Brazil) #116

INGREDIENTS
(Makes 6 servings)
½ chicken, de-boned
2 cups chicken broth
2 cups water
½ lb. fresh shrimp
1 herb bouquet (sage, bay
 leaf and rosemary)
½ lb. fish (preferably tuna or
 sardines)

4 Tbsp. olive oil
1 can hearts of palm
1 tsp. wheat flour
1¼ cup corn flour
1¼ cup manioc flour
2 slices white bread, diced
1 can green peas
2 tomatoes,seeded & diced
2 onions, finely chopped
¼ lb. green olives,sliced

4 cloves garlic, crushed
2 Tbsp. paprika
2 Tbsp. pepper
2 Tbsp. chopped cheiro
 pepper
2 Tbsp. butter
1 can of sardines in oil
4 Tbsp. tomato sauce
6 hardboiled eggs

PREPARATION

FIRST STEP
Boil the chicken in the broth. Cool, take out of the broth and cut in pieces. Set aside.

Boil the shrimp in the water for 15 minutes, together with the herbs.

Cut the fish in pieces and fry it in oil on both sides until golden. Remove from heat, add the chicken, shrimp, thinly sliced hearts of palms, wheat, corn and manioc flours, diced bread slices, and green peas. Finally, add the water that came with the hearts of palms and the peas. Allow to rest for 20 minutes and set aside.

SECOND STEP
Dice the tomatoes, seeded, finely chop the onions, and fry both in butter together with the sliced olives, crushed garlic, paprika, pepper, and cheiro pepper, without membranes or seeds. Set aside.

THIRD STEP
Heat the sardines in the tomato sauce for 5 minutes and set aside.

In a cuscuz dish, spread successive layers of each of the mixtures, alternating with egg slices.

Cover the cuscuz dish, fill the base with water, and steam for 15 minutes over high flame. Serve as an only dish.

NOTE
The water added to the cuscuz dish must reach a high temperature so that its evaporation may facilitate the cooking process.

manioc flour mashed together, and the *buchada de carneiro,* boiled and seasoned innards. Goat (*bode*) is cooked in stews, roasted, or fried. Dendê oil is used in salads and frying on the coast of Bahía. It is also used in *xinxim,* a traditional Afro-Bahían chicken stew. The Northeast's coastal fringe is studded with huts that improvise fish dishes on the beaches.

Bahía and Maranhao are notable in the culinary geography of the Northeast. Some say that the food of Bahía, because it is the result of many mixed cultural contributions, is the real national cuisine, confirmed by their preference for products of the land and with African contributions. Salvador was the colonial capital of Brazil where fruit, vegetables, and spices from the great Portuguese empire were introduced and acclimatized. The people of

Cuxá Rice (Brazil) #117

INGREDIENTS
(Makes 4 servings)
¼ lb. dry shrimp
¼ lb. fresh shrimp
2 green onions

1 onion
2 tomatoes, seeded & diced
1 clove garlic
2 Tbsp. olive oil
2 bunches sorrel

2 tsp. chopped fresh mint
  leaves
½ cup rice, cooked
water as needed
salt

PREPARATION

Peel the dry shrimp and soak in water for an hour. Remove, wash to eliminate excess salt and set aside. Peel the fresh shrimp and cut them in small pieces.

Finely chop the onions and dice the tomatoes, seeded. Fry them in oil for 15 minutes over medium heat, together with the mint leaves, the crushed garlic and the fresh and dry shrimp. Add salt.

Remove from heat and add the sorrel leaves in thin strips; mix well.

Spread over the rice, previously cooked in 10 oz. of hot water for 20 minutes.

Serve hot.

> **NOTE**
> It is better to use young sorrel sprouts, which are less acid.

Bahía flock to their Christian churches and processions while continuing to practice rites and beliefs with African roots. Tourists join in the celebration of Carnival and worship the coconut palm–fringed beaches.

Many of the mouth-watering aromas characteristic of this historic and festive capital of Brazil come from the matrons dressed in white who prepare food on strategic corners in the city. On offer are crabs, fried bananas with cornmeal, *pe-de-moleque* (a type of nougat made with brown sugar), *beiju* (a manioc pancake more rural than urban), and *tapiocas*: velvety, rubbery manioc pancakes with cheese and ground coconut fillings cooked to order on a sheet of tin. *Acarajé* is a small pancake made with feijao fried in dendê oil, served with pepper sauce, onion, and dried shrimp. When the cook herself serves it to you wrapped in banana leaves it is called *abará*.

Shrimp Moqueca *(Brazil)* #*118*

INGREDIENTS
(Makes 4 servings)
1 green pepper
1 red pepper
1½ lb. clean shrimp

1 onion, thinly sliced
2 tsp. olive oil
1 tsp. lemon juice
4 Tbsp. dendê oil
1 Tbsp. coconut milk

3 Tbsp. chopped
  coriander
salt and pepper

PREPARATION

Cut the peppers, without seeds or membranes, into thin strips. Place the shrimp in a pot, cover them with the onion slices and the pepper strips. Pour the olive oil and the lemon juice over them, add salt and pepper and allow to marinate for 30 minutes. Add the dendê oil and cook for 10 minutes over medium heat. Add the coconut milk and continue cooking until it starts to boil.

Serve sprinkled with chopped coriander. Garnish with white rice or pirão.

> **NOTE**
> Pirão: mix sautéed onion with chopped coriander and manioc flour dissolved in cold broth and cook for 10 minutes over low heat, stirring constantly.

At these handy roadside banquets the visitor should try *carurú, vatapá,* and the seafood soups, *moqueca. Carurú* is a stew of *quiabos* (a sort of green bean), meat, or shrimp, seasoned with dendê oil and pepper. This Afro-Brazilian dish, very like Caribbean calulú, is the votive offering for Xangó, one of Bahia's domestic deities (*orixás*). Bahia's vatapá is as nutritious and easily found on the streets as its Belém version. Moqueca is the most ubiquitous dish in Bahian restaurants. It is accompanied by *pirao* (manioc meal boiled in fish stock) and *farofa,* manioc flour with ground meat and dendê oil. Although moqueca is popular along the whole of the Brazilian coast, the natives of Espírito Santo state (*capixabas*) have a patent on this delicious stew. During the Festas Juninas, a June festival very much celebrated all over Brazil, *quentao* is drunk: hot cane liquor or wine mulled with ginger, cinnamon, sugar, and cloves.

In Maranhao state, between the Northeast and Amazonia, rice, fish, and seafood come into their own, prepared as stews (*caldeiradas*), soups

da Barra River,
Arraial, Brazil.

Photo: Rafael Ruiz

Capixaba Cake *(Brazil)* #*119*

INGREDIENTS
(Makes 4 servings)
DOUGH
8 Tbsp. wheat flour
4½ Tbsp. butter
1 Tbsp. yeast
1 egg
1 tsp. salt

FILLING
¼ lb. catfish
1 onion
2 tomatoes
¼ lb. clean mussels
¼ lb. clean oysters
¼ lb. hearts of palms
1 tsp. wheat flour

2 Tbsp. olive oil
1 tsp. dendê oil
juice of one lemon
1 tsp. cumin
2 Tbsp. chopped green
   onion
1 bunch coriander,
   chopped

4 Tbsp. water from the
   hearts of palms
1 egg yolk
1 tsp. pepper
salt
butter as needed (to
   grease the mold)

São Paulo, Brazil.

Photo: Panoramic Images

NOTE
To enhance the striking qualities of this dish, serve it with a fresh vegetable salad.
To open the oysters easily, pry between the shells on the side with a sharp knife to cut the adducent muscle in their centers.

PREPARATION

PIE CRUST

Mix the wheat flour thoroughly with 4 Tbsp. cold butter, yeast and salt. Add the egg and knead until the dough no longer sticks to your hands. Let the dough rest in the fridge, covered with a cloth, for half an hour.

Take out the ball of dough and roll it with a wooden pin to a thickness of ⅕ inch. Cut a 9-inch disc and an 8-inch disc from the dough.

Grease an 8-inch pie dish, and line the bottom and the edges with the larger disc. Pierce the dough with a fork to prevent it from blistering while baking, and pre-cook it at high (425° F) for 10 to 15 minutes.

FILLING

Clean the mussels and the oysters. Set aside. Finely chop the onion and dice the tomatoes, seeded. Sauté them in olive oil for 15 minutes, together with the chopped catfish. Add the mussels and the oysters — whole but shelled — and cook for 10 minutes over low heat. Add the dendê oil, the lemon juice, the green onion, the coriander, the hearts of palms (saving the packing liquid), chopped, and the cumin. Add salt and pepper and continue cooking for another 5 minutes over medium heat.

Mix the water of the hearts of palms with the wheat flour and add it to the mixture, stirring constantly until it thickens. Cook another 5 minutes and allow to cool.

Spread the filling over the pie crust, cover with the remaining disc and brush with the egg yolk, slightly beaten. Bake at high (425° F) until the crust is completely golden, about 15 to 20 minutes.

Serve hot or cold.

(*ensopadas*), and puddings (*budines*). Those in the know assure us that it is one of the most natural and healthy cuisines of Brazil, always using fresh ingredients, moderately seasoned, less fiery than Bahian cooking and reminiscent of Portuguese cooking and sweets. Rice was always the characteristic crop of Maranhao. The most traditional dish is *cuxá*, rice cooked in a sauce made from the leaves of vinagreira, an edible herb. It is not the kind of treat one gets every day. Sao Luis, the historic capital of Maranhao, is known for its colonial houses and some Afro-American feasts, such as Bumba-meu-boi, which survive to this day. During such a weekend the fish restaurants of Sao José de Ribamar are well worth a visit.

Quindim (Brazil) #120

INGREDIENTS
(Makes 6 servings)
1 cup sugar
1 Tbsp. butter

6 egg yolks
2 eggs
2 tsp. vanilla extract
½ fresh grated coconut

sugar and butter as
needed (for the pan)

PREPARATION

Beat the sugar and the butter with an electric beater for 5 minutes until creamy. Gradually add the yolks, one at a time, stirring constantly. Add the eggs, the vanilla extract and finally the grated coconut, always stirring the mixture to combine all the ingredients well.

Grease and cover a 9-inch tube pan with sugar. Pour the mixture in it and place the tube pan in another pan filled with water. Preheat the oven for 10 minutes at medium temperature (350º F) and bake the quindim in it for another 20 minutes.

Remove, cool and unmold while still warm, since the sugar hardens when cold, sticking to the walls of the container.

NOTE
The eggs and egg yolks must be at room temperature.
If you are using a wire beater, the sugar and butter must be beaten for 10 minutes.

For many, it is in the kitchens of Minas Gerais that the most appetizing national flavors converge. Here pork and chicken are dignified with tasty sauces and accompaniments: *farofa* (a favorite vegetable in Brazil), *quiabo* (the fruit of a vegetable originally from Angola), *ora-pro-nobis* (a local vegetable), and *angú* (the native cornmeal adapted to the diet of African slaves). In historic cities restaurants offer chicken *caipira* with quiabo and angú, and *tutu-à-mineira* (a feijoada made with chitterlings, miners' sausage, pork, couve vegetable, and feijao), accompanied by fried eggs, banana, angú, and manioc flour. Everyone recommends dulce de leche with coconut, jaboticaba fruit jellies, and the cheese from Serro, a delightful town in the old diamond-bearing mountains. Coffee comes with *quitandas,* a term

Pará Cake *(Brazil)* #*121*

INGREDIENTS
(Makes 8 servings)
CRUST
1 Tbsp. butter
1 Tbsp. sugar
2 Tbsp. grated pará chestnuts
¼ lb. wheat flour
butter as needed (to grease the pan)

FROSTING
⅓ cup butter, softened
½ cup. sugar
1 egg yolk
1 tsp. vanilla extract

2 Tbsp. roasted pará chestnuts, grated

PREPARATION

CRUST
Beat the butter and sugar until creamy; add the pará chestnuts. Add the wheat flour and mix without stopping to form a homogeneous dough. Wrap it in wax paper and let it rest in the fridge for an hour.

Grease a 10-inch pan. Roll the dough to ¼-inch thickness, cover the pan and bake it in a pre-heated oven at medium (350º F). Bake for about 35 minutes until the crust is golden.

Remove, cool, unmold and cover with the cream.

FROSTING
Beat the butter at room temperature with the sugar, egg yolk and vanilla extract until you get a white cream.

Place the cream in a decorator bag with a smooth tip and make lines forming a checkerboard. Fill the places corresponding to the dark squares with the grated roasted chestnuts.

NOTE
Toast the chestnuts on an ungreased cookie sheet at medium for 20 minutes.

Cozido Bahiano *(Brazil)* #122

INGREDIENTS
(Makes 6 servings)
¼ lb. jerk beef
½ lb. flank or brisket
1 qt. water
¼ lb. pork tongue

¼ lb. bacon
2 German sausages
½ lb. chicken breast
2 onions, quartered
2 tomatoes, quartered
¼ lb. squash, cut up

1 bouquet of herbs
  (sage, rosemary and
  thyme)
¼ lb. okra
¼ lb. cucumbers in
  brine

¼ lb. white cabbage
2 bananas
4 sweet potatoes
¼ lb. sweet manioc
1¼ lb. manioc flour
salt

PREPARATION

Soak the jerk beef in water for two hours to eliminate excess salt. Set aside.

In a quart of water, place the flank or brisket, cut in three chunks, together with the jerk beef, halved, and boil for an hour over high heat. Add salt and put in the pork tongue, previously peeled and cut in chunks, the bacon, the sausages, and the chicken breast. Quarter the onions and the tomatoes, seeded, and cut the squash in pieces. Add the onions, the tomatoes and the squash together with the herbs, the okra and the cucumbers. Lower the heat to medium and continue cooking for 30 minutes.

Add the cabbage, the bananas, and the sweet potatoes and sweet manioc, both peeled and quartered. Continue cooking over medium heat, covered, for 30 minutes.

Boil the manioc flour in 2 ladlefuls of the cooking broth over medium heat, stirring constantly with a wooden spoon until it thickens, approximately 20 minutes.

Serve the meats, the vegetables and the manioc flour in separate dishes, allowing guests to serve themselves.

> NOTE
> Salt sparingly, for the jerk beef and the bacon contain a lot of salt.

Lomo Mineiro *(Brazil)* #*123*

INGREDIENTS
(Makes 4 servings)
2 lb. pork loin
2 cloves garlic
1 tsp. ground pepper
6 peppercorns
2 bay leaves

2 tsp. vinegar
salt
2 Tbsp. dry white wine
2 Tbsp. lard
1 onion
1 green onion
1 green pepper

1 tsp. cumin

GARNISH
1½ cups white rice
1 qt. vegetable broth
2 Tbsp. chopped
  parsley

lemon slices for
  decoration

FAROFA
1 onion
¼ cup butter
7 oz. manioc flour

Thoroughly mix the crushed garlic, the ground pepper and the peppercorns, the bay leaf and the vinegar. Salt to taste and cover the loin on both sides with the mixture. Allow to marinate in the fridge for 2 to 3 hours.

Pour the wine over the loin and continue marinating in the fridge for another 2 hours.

Remove from the marinade, rub the loin with one Tbsp. lard and cook in oven at medium (350° F) for 45 minutes. Set aside.

Finely chop the two kinds of onions and the pepper, without seeds or membranes. Fry them together with the cumin in the remaining lard, over medium heat, for 10 minutes.

Remove, cover the loin with this mixture on both sides, and raise the oven temperature to high, cooking for approximately 10 minutes. Take out of the oven, slice and place on a serving dish. Sprinkle with chopped parsley and decorate with lemon slices.

Serve with white rice cooked in vegetable broth, or with farofa.

FAROFA

Finely chop the onion and fry it in butter for 5 minutes over medium heat. Finely sprinkle the manioc flour into it, stirring constantly with a wooden spoon, and continue cooking over medium heat for 10 minutes, until it blends in with the rest.

---

used in Minas for tasty homemade pastries, though in other regions it refers to fruit. To get an idea of the ingredients used in Minas cooking one should visit the market at Belo Horizonte. This state capital is the departure point for a trip along the "Cachaça Road." Before it became the drink of wayside pubs, *cachaça* (the Brazilian rum) was used medicinally as one of the components in the treatment for snake-bite. In Sao Joao de el Rey there is a Rua da Cachaça (Cachaça Street). Caipirinha is the most famous drink made with this rum, plus tiny, crushed aromatic lemons and sugar, to be drunk on the beaches by tourists or as an aperitif before feijoada.

Goiás Velho, the former capital of Goiás state, is one of the towns that has kept its colonial atmosphere best. There the typical dishes are *empadao* and *pamonha.* Goiás' empadao is a small but nutritious pie stuffed with chicken, pork, sausage meat, fresh peas, egg, olives, and the local *palmito* (heart of palm) called *guariroba.* Pamonha is a Brazilian version of the

Coconut Rocambole (Brazil) #124

INGREDIENTS
(Makes 6 servings)
½ lb. grated coconut
1 Tbsp. butter
1 Tbsp. wheat flour
3 Tbsp. sugar
4 egg yolks
4 egg whites
1 tsp. cinnamon powder
2 tsp. confectioner's sugar
butter as needed (to grease the mold)

PREPARATION

Beat the egg yolks and 2 Tbsp. of sugar with a wire beater for 10 minutes. Set aside.

Beat the egg whites separately for 10 minutes until they form peaks. Add them to the egg yolk mixture, blending them with a rubber spatula with slow upward movements, bringing the mixture up from the bottom. Add the melted butter, at room temperature, the sifted flour and finally the coconut, sprinkling it finely; stir softly but constantly at each addition with a spatula.

Grease a cookie sheet, cover the base with waxed paper, pour the mixture over it and spread it evenly with a long spatula.

Cook at medium (350° F) for 10 minutes, until the surface begins to brown slightly.

Remove from the oven, unmold on a cloth sprinkled with the remaining sugar and the cinnamon and roll with the help of the cloth.

Remove the cloth, cut the roll in small slices and sprinkle with the confectioner's sugar.

NOTE
In order for the mixture not to stick to the cloth it is better to moisten the latter lightly.

Spanish-American tamale, wrapped in corn husks. Every village in Goiás, however humble, has a *pamonharia*. The people of Goiás, like those of Minas Gerais, are devotees of sweet things. Cora Coralina, the poetess from Goiás, had a sweet tooth.

Mato Grosso cuisine is based on local fish and roast meat. Plantains are used in preparing dishes both salty and sweet. The tail of the cayman is still appreciated. In times past, when hunting and fishing provided food for inland Brazil, it was common to buy cayman in the markets, but extensive cattle-raising gave people a taste for beef. On the tourist *estancias* (large cattle farms) in the Pantanal (an immense floodable plain that is one of the world's havens for wildlife), dorado, pacú, and pintado fish are caught and

Ambrosía (Brazil) #125

INGREDIENTS
(Makes 4 servings)
4 egg yolks
2 egg whites

2 cups milk
1 Tbsp. sugar
1 tsp. cinnamon powder
1 whole clove

rind of one lemon
rind of one orange

PREPARATION

Beat the egg yolks until creamy. Beat the whites separately until they form peaks, adding them slowly and gradually to the yolks with a soft, blending motion. Set aside.

Mix the milk, sugar, cinnamon, clove, and lemon and orange rinds, and simmer for 40 minutes until the mixture thickens and is reduced to half of its volume. Discard the rinds

Add the mixture of yolks and whites and continue cooking without stirring, over low heat, for 5 minutes, until the yolks and whites are cooked.

At that point, using a wooden spoon, bring up the lower part of the mixture to break through the egg mixture.

Remove from heat, allow to cool and refrigerate for 2 hours. Serve very cold in stem glasses.

NOTE
Heat the milk with the sugar and the rest of the ingredients, without allowing it to boil, stirring constantly with a wooden spoon to prevent the mixture from sticking to the bottom of the pot.

prepared in the oven, on the grill, or in stews. The local hands (*boadeiros*) cook cows' heads stuffed and roasted while they drink *mate*.

Paulistas (the people of Sao Paulo) assure us that nowhere in Brazil — even in South America — is food as good as in that city. Tour guides mention over thirty different dishes. Typical of Sao Paulo is *cuscuz*. Both the Portuguese and Africans arrived knowing all about couscous but the local version is somewhat different, being prepared with corn (not sorghum), and served as a pie in a special dish called *cuscuzeira*, often with coconut milk. Food bought by the kilo satisfies those who need to eat in a hurry but still prefer a table, without having to descend to hamburgers and fries. In this way one can buy helpings of cooked dishes suited to the taste and

Brigadeiros (Brazil) #*126*

INGREDIENTS
(Makes 4 servings)
1 can condensed milk
¼ lb. powdered cocoa

¼ lb. grated unsweetened chocolate
1 Tbsp. margarine
¼ lb. seedless black raisins
1 shot rum

PREPARATION

Boil the unopened can of condensed milk in water for 30 minutes; let it cool. Open the can, pour its contents in a pot, add the cocoa and half a Tbsp. of margarine and mix. Cook over medium heat for 10 minutes, stirring constantly with a wooden spoon, until the spoon leaves a furrow as it scrapes the bottom of the pot.

Grease a mold with the remaining margarine and pour the mixture in it. Chill for 10 hours.

Soak the raisins in rum for an hour, drain and set aside.

Remove the mold from the fridge, take small portions with a spoon, add one or two raisins to each, and form them into 1½-inch balls.

Roll the balls on grated unsweetened chocolate and serve in small fluted paper bonbon cups.

> **NOTE**
> You will know you have reached the desired consistency when you see the furrow form in the bottom of the pot as you scrape it with the spoon.

Cream Biscuits (Brazil) #127

INGREDIENTS
(Makes 6 servings)
1 cup whipping cream
2 Tbsp. butter
3 egg yolks

4 Tbsp. sugar
1 Tbsp. powdered yeast
cornstarch as needed
butter as needed (to grease the mold)
¼ tsp. salt

PREPARATION

Beat the butter with the sugar until creamy; add the yolks, one at a time, and mix well until the mixture is homogeneous. Add the yeast, whipping cream, salt, and cornstarch as needed, kneading continuously until the dough no longer sticks to your hands.

Cut small portions, roll them to form 2-inch long cylinders, ¾ inch in diameter, and pinch the ends together to form rings.

Grease a cookie sheet, place the biscuits on it and bake at medium (350º F) for 15 minutes.

> **NOTE**
> Sift the cornstarch to prevent it from lumping and make it easier to work into the dough.

A dwelling by the
Amazon River,
Para, Brazil.

appetite of the consumer. The better examples of these food shops in Sao
Paulo employ nutritionists and professional chefs.

South from Sao Paulo the immigrants' cuisine was adapted to tropical
climes and to what the land produced, thus stimulating new eating habits.
Here the fishermen's traditional recipes are found side by side with the
meats produced on cattle *fazendas* (farms) with other ingredients from
Brazilian cuisine. German settlers brought their sausages, dairy products,
smoked meats, sweets; Italians their pizzas, pastas, *galetos* (roast chicken),
and wine. On Santa Catarina's coast one can find habits and tastes adapted by and for the waves of Argentine visitors who yearly descend on the
beaches of Florianópolis.

Rio Grande do Sul is the land of the gaúcho steak. At Brazilian barbecues
the cook brings those cuts he considers "à point" to the table on a sword-
like *espeto* and there and then slices off the bits chosen. Though no roast
meat is offered without salads, these barbecues may be the only case in
Brazil where only one ingredient is served. No seasoning is allowed to
alter the flavor of the meat except salt. Rio Grande do Sul produces the
best of Brazilian wines; consumption is increasing and quality improving.

Siricaia (Brazil) #128

INGREDIENTS
(Makes 4 servings)

8 slices white bread
1 Tbsp. butter, melted
¾ lb. soft cheese, sliced
3 eggs
3 Tbsp. sugar
1 qt. milk
1 Tbsp. cinnamon powder

PREPARATION

Cut the crust off the bread slices and place them in a glass casserole dish.

Brush them evenly with the melted butter, cover with slices of soft cheese and set aside.

Beat the eggs with the sugar, milk and cinnamon. Pour over the bread slices and the cheese, making sure the egg and milk mixture gets soaked into the bread.

Bake at high (425º F) for 15 minutes, until the cheese has melted. Remove from the oven, cut in 2½-inch squares and serve hot.

> **NOTE**
> In order to get an airy, creamy mixture, the eggs should be at room temperature; beat them with the sugar using an electric beater for 15 minutes.

Recipe Glossary (Brazil)

CACHAÇA: rum.

CASQUINHAS: shells.

CHEIRO PEPPER: small, hot red pepper.

DENDÊ: palm tree, up to 50 feet high, from whose fruit dendê oil is extracted.

FAROFA: manioc flour mixed with onions, egg or butter.

GUARANÁ: fruit of the guaranezeiro, a typical tree of western Amazonia, a great stimulant.

JAMBÚ: typical plant of the north of Brazil. It contains spicy substances.

JERK BEEF: dry, cured beef; it must be soaked in abundant water to eliminate excess salt and hydrate.

MOQUECA: fish stew.

OKRA: Arabic beans.

PIRÃO: the mixture of broth and manioc flour, used as a side dish to accompany many dishes.

SORREL: aromatic plant with thick, rounded leaves and acid flavor, used as a condiment and also in salads.

Glossary of Latin American Cooking Terms

Abacate (BR): aguacate (ME) avocado "pear".

Açaí (BR): fruit of an Amazonian palm.

Achiote: seed used for coloring food.

Achuras (AR): innards often served with roast beef.

Agüita (CH): herb tea.

Ají: small chili pepper.

Ajiaco (CO, CU): meat and vegetable soup.

Ajonjolí: sesame.

Alfeñique: cooked sugar paste rolled out.

Almojábana (CO): cornmeal, cheese, and egg croquette used as wheat-bread in the Colombian Andes.

Ananás: pineapple. The name comes from its being shaped like a pine cone.

Antojito (ME): aperitif, snack or side dish of fried corn tortillas.

Arepa (CO, VE): cornmeal tortilla baked or cooked on a griddle.

Arrope: must of boiled fruit which reaches sirupy consistency.

Asado (AR): barbecued meat and innards.

Asado de tira (AR): rib-roast cooked on the grill.

Asado negro (VE): meat roasted in the oven with brown sugar.

Asadura: innards used in barbecues.

Asopao (PR, RD): chicken with rice.

Atol (CU): paste made with fermented tender cornmeal and sugar.

Atole (ME): drink made from cornmeal soaked in milk or water, sweetened and flavored with brown sugar and cinnamon.

Azul-marinho (BR): fish casserole with cooked, fermented plantains.

Banana: plantains eaten raw.

Bandeirantes (BR): expeditionaries from Sao Paulo who penetrated the interior in search of slaves and gold.

Barbacoa (ME): meats and vegetables cooked underground with hot stones.

Barbacoa: Caribbean grill. Meat cooked on the grill.

Barreado (BR): meat stew.

Batata: sweet potato or yam.

Beiju (BR): tortilla of manioc flour and grated coconut wrapped in banana leaves.

Bife (AR): steak.

Bife de chorizo (AR): sirloin steak.

Bijao (CO): leaf for wrapping tamales.

Birrias (ME): roast goat.

Bolinho (BR): meatballs.

Bollo (CO): elongated croquette wrapped in corn husk.

Bucaneros: hunters of wildlife who smoked wild pig over wooden grills (*boucan*) and sold the smoked meat (*viande boucanée*) to passing shipas and pirates.

Buñuelo: fritters of flour.

Cabrito (CO, CH): young goat.

Cacahuate, cacahuete: peanuts.

Cachaza, cachaça: Brazilian rum.

Caipirinha (BR): drink made of cachaça, aromatic lemons and sugar.

Cajeta (ME): burnt milk caramel.

Cajú: cashew, native to Central America and northeast Brazil.

Calalú, calalou, callaloo: Afro-Caribbean soup.

Calabaza: pumpkin.

Caldeirada (BR): fish and seafood stew.

Caldillo (ME): stock with ground meat. (BO, CH) stock with fish and seafood.

Callos: tripe.

Camote (PE, EC, ME): sweet potato, yam.

Candomblé (BR): a religion from Bahia, with Yoruba roots.

Cañazo (PE): sugar-cane juice (fermented).

Capia (AR): toasted tender corn flour.

Carapulcra (PE): ancient way of cooking by putting hot stones in the pot. Potato stew.

Cardápio (BR): menu.

Carimañola (CO): fried cassava bun.

Carnita (ME): bits of fried pork, seasoned.

Carurú (BR): Afro-Brazilian casserole, the name from a plant the leaves of which are tasty and nutritious.

Casabe, cazabe: manioc flour tortilla. Cassava bread.

Cazuela (CH): a Chilean dish.

Cebiche, ceviche: macerated fish eaten raw.

Cecina (PA): salt-beef, jerked meat.

Chala (AR, BO): corn husk used to wrap humitas and tamales.

Chancaca (AR, BO, PE): sugarcane molasses, brown sugar.

Chapulín (ME): edible crickets.

Charqui: strips of sun- or air-dried meat, jerky.

Chayote: Antillean squash.

Chicha: pre-Columbian "beer" made from fermented corn. There are many kinds, using different cereals or fruit and in the degree of fermentation.

Chicha morada (PE, BO): chicha made from wine-red corn.

Chicharrón: ground fat done to a crisp; chitterlings.

Chile: hot peppers.

Chimarrao (BR): hot "mate" drink.

Chimichurri (AR): a barbecue sauce for roast meats and innards.

Chinchulín (BO, AR, UR): small intestines of beef or sheep.

Chipá, chipa (PA, AR): buns made of manioc flour and cheese.

Chipilín (GU, ME, ES): leguminous plant.

Choclo: corn on the cob.

Chuño, chuñu (AR, BO, PE): dehydrated potato.

Chupe (PE): fish or meat stews.

Churrasco (BR): barbecue roast.

Churrasquera (UR): fire-pit and grill to roast meat.

Cimarrón (AR): old name for unsweetened "mate.".

Cimarrón: name for escaped slaves living in the woods. Their subsistence foods definitely influenced the preparation of certain regional foods.

Coalhada (BR): junket or homemade yoghurt.

Cocada (BR): nougat made with ground coconut and molasses.

Cocido: meat and vegetables boiled together.

Coriandro: coriander.

Cuchuco (CO): stock as made in the Colombian Andes.

Curanto (CH): Araucanian dish typical of Chiloë Island, based on seafood, meat and vegetables cooked over hot stones in a pit.

Dendê (BR): a palm oil.

Dulce de leche: caramel made with milk and sugar long boiled.

Dumplings: Caribbean croquettes.

Elote (CO, VE, ME, EC): corn on the cob.

Empanada: pasty with various fillings.

Enchiladas (ME, GU): cornmeal tortillas rolled to contain chili and meat, later baked.

Escamoles (ME): edible ant eggs (Mexico's caviar).

Fanesca (EC): soup or stew made with dried fish, grain and legumes, traditionally an Easter dish.

Fariña: manioc flour.

Farofa (BR): manioc flour toasted with shredded meat.

Fazenda (BR): farm.

Frijol, fríjol, frejol: dried beans.

Fufú (CU): mashed green plantains with chitterlings and a nutritious tuber.

Garífunas, garifas (BE, GU, HO): descendants of black slaves and indigenous Caribs living on the Gulf of Honduras.

Guaguas (PE): pan dulce.

Guajolote (ME): Mexican turkey.

Guañaca (CH): pork stock with cornmeal.

Guaraná (BR): an Amazon fruit. Popular fizzy drink.

Guarapo: "beer" made from sugarcane.

Guaschalocro (AR): stew of cracked corn and pumpkin, called "poor man's locro" because it has no meat.

Guata, guatitas (CH, EC, PE): tripe, cow's stomach.

Hallaca (CO, VE): a sort of tamale wrapped in banana leaves.

Hogao, hogo (CO): lightly fried and basted.

Huarique (PE): hiding place.

Huevos pericos: scrambled eggs.

Huitlacoche, cuitlacoche (ME): edible parasitic fungus of corn.

Humita, huminta: boiled sweetcorn kernels, ground and seasoned, worked into a paste.

Jambú (BR): peppery-hot plant from the north.

Jerk (JA): an escaped slaves' way of cooking and seasoning meat and fish.

Jitomate (ME): red (ripe) tomato (versus green tomato).

Judías pintas: red beans.

Kebbe: croquette of stewed ground meat, from Arabian cookery.

Lagua (BO): thick soup.

Locoto, locote (BO): chili pepper.

Locro: thick stew of cracked corn, meats, pumpkin, potatoes, etc.

Llapingachos (EC): cheese and potato omelette.

Majarete (CU, RD): paste of ground corn, milk, cinnamon, and grated lemon rind.

Malanga: nutritious tuber. "Calalú" is made from its leaves.

Mamao (BR): pawpaw, papaya.

Mamey: fruit of the zapote tree.

Mamona (CO): veal.

Mandioca: manioc.

Maniçoba (BR): Amazonian preparation from the boiled poisonous leaves of manioc, pork, saussage, and bacon.

Manjar, manjar blanco: milk caramel.

Maracuyá: fruit of the passión flower.

Mate (AR, CH, PA, UR): local "green" tea; gourd from which it is drunk.

Mazamorra: cracked corn boiled with sweetened milk.

Metate (GU, ME): grinding stone.

Mezcal (ME): spirit made from mead of the agave.

Milho (BR): corn, sweet corn, corn on the cob.

Mojito (CU): cocktail with lemon juice, rum, ground ice, soda water and a sprig of mint.

Mole (ME): thick sauce of chili and spices, typìcal of Mexican cooking.

Mondongo (AR): cow's stomach for stews, callos in Spain, guatitas in Chile. In Colombia and other countries it might include intestines.

Moqueca (BR): sea-food or fish stew.

Moquém (BR): native Brazilian barbecue. Primitive grill for cooking or smoking meats and fish.

Moro, moros: rice and beans in various Central American countries.

Mosto (PA): sugar-cane juice.

Mote (AR): peeled corn boiled to a mush with ash; traditional stew.

Mote (EC): a type of tasteless corn.

Mote (CO): cooked peeled corn. Thick mush of tubers (yams) or fruit (hearts of palm, bananas) cooked and mashed, mixed with milk.

Nogada: dish or sauce prepared with nuts.

Nopal (ME): a cactus.

Ñame: yam, tuber like a sweet potato

Octli (ME): Aztec wine which spaniards called "pulque".

Ocopa (PE): sauce made with seasoned chili peppers, peanuts, garlic and onion which goes with shrimps and other dishes.

Olla podrida: meat and vegetables boiled together.

Once, onces (CO, CH): snack

Orixá (BR): Afro-Brazilian deity.

Pachamanca (PE): food traditionally offered to Pachamama.

Paila marina (CH): sea-food stock with a piece of conger eel.

Palta (AR, PE): avocado.

Pamplona (UR): pork stuffed with ham and cheese, roasted on the grill.

Panceta (AR): bacon.

Panelada (BR): casserole.

Panqueque (AR): stuffed crepe.

Pão de queijo (BR): cornmeal and cheese bun.

Papa: potato; South American tuber; many varieties are used.

Papa dulce: sweet potato.

Papaya: pawpaw.

Pargo: fish much appreciated in Caribbean cooking.

Parrilla (AR): fire-pit and grill.

Parrillada (AR, PA): grilled meats; meat restaurant.

Patacón (EC): "green" plantain thickly sliced and fried.

Pebre (CH): barbecue sauce with coriander.

Peixada (BR): casserole of vegetables and portions of fresh fish, coriander and coconut milk.

Pequi, piqui (BR): aromatic fruit from the savannahs relished as an accompaniment for rice or chicken stew.

Picoso: "hot."

Piloncillo (ME): brown sugar.

Pimienta de Jamaica: Jamaica pepper, for seasoning soups, pickles, deserts and liqueurs.

Pimiento: chili peppers — pods

eaten raw, cooked, or dry, ground as a spice. "hot" or not, but nothing to do with pepper (corns). Aztecs called them chilis.

Piña: pineapple.

Pirão (BR): manioc flour mush prepared with fish stock.

Pisco (PE): spirit distilled from skins and pips of trodden grapes.

Pitahaya: prickly pear.

Plátano (VE): plantain; cooking banana.

Plátano macho (CU): banana for frying.

Plateada (CH): meat casserole.

Puchero: stewed meat and vegetables, *cozido* in Portuguese, *pot-au-feu* in French.

Pulmay (CH): *curanto* done in a pot.

Pulque (ME): rum made from agave, *octli* to pre-Hispanic Mexicans.

Putaparió (AR): chili pepper.

Quesadillas (ME): corn-flour pancakes filled with stew or cheese.

Quiabo (BR): hibiscus-like pod.

Quimbombó, quingombó: legume much appreciated in traditional Afro-Cuban dishes.

Quincho (AR): barbecue thatched shelter where the grill is and the meats are cooked.

Quinua, quinoa: highly nutritious Andean cereal; part of the Inca diet.

Rapadura (BR): brown sugar tablets.

Revuelto gramajo (AR): eggs scrambled with chopped ham and fried potatos.

Rocoto (PE): peppers.

Ron, rum, rhum: rum; in the Caribbean from distilled sugar-cane.

Sajta (AR, BO): spicy stew of ground jerky or chicken.

Sancocho, sancochado: meat and vegetables boiled together.

Seco (CO, EC, VE, PE): main dish of the meal, meat stew.

Seco de carne (PE): jerked llama meat or mutton.

Seco de chivo (EC): goat or mutton cooked with rice.

Sopaipillas (BO): flattened bread dough fried.

Surullitos (PR): fried tidbits.

Taco (ME): thin corn pancakes filled with stew, chilis, cheese, etc.

Tamales: cornmeal cooked in corn husks or banana leaves.

Tasajo: strips of sun-dried beef.

Tequila (ME): spirit from agave.

Tereré (BR, PA): cold "mate" infusion.

Ternero, ternera (AR): veal, the best cuts for barbecue.

Tianquis, tianguiz (ME): Meso-American public market usually in a plaza.

Tinga (ME): shredded and stewed beef.

Tlacoyos (ME): cornmeal pancakes filled with beans and chitterlings.

Tortilla (AR): Spanish omlette (with potato, chard, brain).

Tortilla (ME): flat cornmeal "cake".

Tostada (ME): cornmeal tortilla fried to spread with meat, beans, or sauces. Slice of toast.

Tostado (AR, EC): toasted or fried corn. Sandwich toasted to order.

Tostones (CO, CU, VE): fried "green" plantains.

Tucupí (BR): seasoning prepared on the basis of poisonous manioc leaves.

Vianda (CU): tropical roots, bananas, pumpkins and potatos for a soup.

Vino patero (AR): home-made wine.

Vodú, vudú (HA): popular imported slave religion — voodoo.

Yuca: manioc.

Zapallo: pumpkin.

Zapote, sapote (ME): fruit of sapote tree. Red mamey. Loquat.

Bibliography

Historia natural y moral de los alimentos. Maguelonne Toussaint-Samat. Alianza Editorial. Madrid, 1991.

La fisiología del gusto. J. A. Brillat-Savarin. Zeus. Barcelona, 1970.

Historia de la gastronomía. María Mestayer de Echagüe. Espasa-Calpe. Madrid, 1943.

La cocina cristiana de Occidente. Alvaro Cunqueiro. Tusquets. Colección Los 5 Sentidos. Barcelona, 1991.

La cocina de los antropólogos. Jessica Kuper (recopilación). Tusquets Editores. Colección Los 5 Sentidos. Barcelona, 1984.

Historia real y fantástica del Nuevo Mundo. Horacio J. Becco (selección, prólogo y notas bibliográficas). Biblioteca Ayacucho. Caracas, 1992.

Un banquete para los dioses. Agustín Remesal. Alianza Editorial. Madrid, 1993.

Frutas comestíveis da Amazônia. Paulo B.Cavalcante. CEJUP-Museu Paraense Emílio Goeldi. Belém, 1991.

Frutas de América tropical y subtropical. Clara Inés Olaya. Grupo Editor Norma. Bogotá, 1991.

Especias exóticas. R. Richardson. José J. de Olañeta, Editor. Palma de Mallorca, 1987.

Tradiciones mexicanas. Sebastián Verti. Editorial Diana. México, 1993.

Alimentos de México. Janet Long Solís, Ana María Carrillo, Felipe Solís, Ernesto Velázquez, Ana M.de Benítez. Editorial Clío. México, 1999.

Historia de las Antillas. J. H. Parry y Philip Sherlock. Editorial Kapelusz. Buenos Aires, 1976.

El Caribe. Un Paraíso culinario. Rosemary Parkinson (texto y edición). Könemann. Barcelona, 1999.

La cocina cubana. Un sabor mestizo. Silvia Caunedo. Alianza Editorial. Madrid, 1999.

El sabor de Colombia. Benjamín Villegas (dirección), Antonio Montaña (textos). Villegas Editores. Bogotá, 1997.

Gran libro de la cocina colombiana. Carlos Ordóñez (compilador). Círculo de Lectores-Instituto Colombiano de Cultura. Bogotá, 1984.

Historia y sabor de 30 siglos de la cocina peruana. Autores varios. Universidad San Martín de Porres. Lima, 1999.

Cocina ecléctica. Juana Manuela Gorriti. Librería Sarmiento. Buenos Aires, 1977.

Enciclopedia del folclore de Chile. Manuel Dannemann. Editorial Universitaria. Santiago, 1998.

Guía del buen comer. César Fredes. Fundación para la Innovación Agraria-LOM Ediciones. Santiago, 1999.

Los sabores de la patria. Víctor Ego Ducrot. Grupo Editorial Norma. Buenos Aires, 1998.

A la mesa. Ritos y retos de la alimentación argentina. Marcelo Alvarez y Luisa Pinotti. Grijalbo. Buenos Aires, 2000.

História da vida privada no Brasil. Autores varios. Companhia Das Letras. São Paulo, 1997.

História da alimentaçao no Brasil. Luis da Camara Cascudo. Editora Itatiaia-Editora da Universidade de São Paulo. Belo Horizonte, 1983.

RECIPE BIBLIOGRAPHY

Cocina Mexicana. 101 recetas auténticas de América Central. Roger Hicks.

Cocina Mexicana. Selección de recetas del arte. Mario Antonio Sánchez. Diana, 1991.

El libro clásico de la cocina mexicana. De los antojitos a los postres, las recetas más suculentas de la cocina mexicana. Promesa, 1991.

Alimentos de México, Clío, 1999.

El libro de la cocina latinoamericana. Elisabeth Lambert Ortiz.

El gran libro de la gastronomia colombiana. Julián Estrada Ochoa.

O Sabor do Brasil. Ofelia. DBA/Melhoramentos, 1996.

Magia da Cozinha Brasilera Antonio Hovaiss. Alaim Draeger.

Fogao de Lenha. María Stella Libanio Christo.

Alimentos frescos, Perú el Dorado. La base de la Buena Cocina. Mariano Valderrama.

El reino de los crudos. Antonio Cisneros.

Gran Libro de la Cocina Argentina. Círculo de Lectores, 1985.

La Cocina del Fin del Mundo. Patagonia y Tierra del Fuego. Libros/Books, 2000.

Cocina de Costa Rica. Marjorie Ross de Cerdas.

Cocina Nacional Guatemalteca. Aurora Sierra Franco de Alvarez.

Mesas de Bolivia. Sandra Cattan Naslausky, Rita del Solar.

Gran Libro de la Cocina Chilena. Editorial Bibliográfica Chilena Ltda.

Tetagua Remb'u —Relatos y Recetas—. Ana María Rivarola Matto.

El Caribe. Un Paraíso culinario. Rosemary Parkinson (texto y edición). Könemann. Barcelona, 1999.

Acknowledgements

A Cristina Velázquez, Aurora Montaño Barbosa, Diego Eidelman, Federico Bertero, Guadalupe Peralta y Simon Gutiérrez, Marcos Pícolo, Juliana Orihuela, Doracy Ribeiro, Salvador Gargiulo, Ernestina Fernández, Karime Janen Khouri, Pabla Espínola, Hilda López, Adolfo Linardi, Lautaro Lafleur.

Oficinas culturales y bibliotecas de las embajadas de países latinoamericanos en Buenos Aires: Chile, Colombia, Cuba, Ecuador, Honduras, México, Nicaragua, Panamá, Perú, R. O. del Uruguay, Venezuela.

List of Recipes